FACING AND OVERCOMING
ADVERSITY

Copyright © 2026 by Martin Freeman.

ISBN (eBook/Kindle): 978-1-968012-92-2

ISBN (Paperback): 978-1-968012-93-9

ISBN (Hardcover): 978-1-968012-94-6

Library Of Congress Catalog Card Number: 2026905372

All rights reserved. No part of this book may be reproduced or transmitted in any form or by any means, electronic or mechanical, including photocopying, recording, or by any information storage and retrieval system without express written permission from the author, except in the case of brief quotations embodied in critical reviews and certain other noncommercial uses permitted by copyright law.

Published in the United States of America by Lynx Publishers.

FACING AND OVERCOMING ADVERSITY

A STRATEGIC APPROACH TO BUILDING K-12 RESILIENT STUDENTS

MARTIN FREEMAN

This book is dedicated to the incredible teachers, administrators, support staff, students, and families of the Youngstown City School District. Your resilience, love, courage, compassion, and unwavering belief in what's possible for our students make all the difference.

TABLE OF CONTENTS

Foreword	vi
Preface	xv
Introduction	18
Chapter 1 – The Meaning of Resilience	20
Chapter 2 – Why the Science of Resilience Matters	27
Chapter 3 – The Nature and Nurture of Resilience	33
Chapter 4 – Why Is Resilience Important	39
Chapter 5 – The Foundations of Resilience	47
Chapter 6 – Identifying and Understanding Risk and Protective Factors	54
Chapter 7 – Adversity as A Teacher: Understanding How Adversity Shapes Resilience	64
Chapter 8 – Educator Resilience: The Heartbeat of a Thriving School	68
Chapter 9 – Resilience as a necessity in Today's Educational Climate	76
Chapter 10 – Teaching Student's to Name Their Feelings and Needs	82
Chapter 11 – Creating A Resilient Classroom Environment	87
Chapter 12 – What Resilient Students Do Differently: Profiles, Patterns, and Practices	95
Chapter 13 – Rewriting the Story: Teaching Students to Challenge False Narratives	100
Chapter 14 – Growth Mindset and How It Influences Resilience	105
Chapter 15 – Hope: Teaching Students to See Possibility	110
Chapter 16 – From Struggle to Strength: How Students Grow Beyond Adversity	122
Chapter 17 – The Need for Resilience-Based Interventions for Students	129
Chapter 18 – Profiles in Resilience	135
Acknowledgements	151
About the Author	152
References	153

FOREWORD

"Resilience is not a construct, I encountered first in research or professional learning. It is something I learned through experience; through challenge, responsibility, and the weight of leading in moments where outcomes mattered deeply for children, families, and communities.

My journey in education, from the classroom to district leadership, has been shaped by adversity and sustained by purpose. In urban education especially, resilience is not a supplemental skill. It is foundational. That is precisely why Facing and Overcoming Life's Adversities: A Strategic Approach to Building K–12 Resilient Students is both timely and necessary.

Dr. Martin Freeman's work stands at the intersection of scholarship, practice, and moral leadership. He approaches resilience not as an abstract psychological concept, but as a systemic responsibility of schools ;especially those serving students and communities that have historically carried the greatest burden of inequity. His scholarship is rigorous, grounded in research, and deeply informed by the realities of K–12 education. Just as importantly, his writing reflects a profound respect for educators and students whose lived experiences often go unrecognized in policy conversations.

On a personal level, Dr. Freeman's work resonates with me because it mirrors what I have come to understand through years of service in urban school systems: resilience is built, sustained, and either strengthened or eroded by the systems we design. His work affirms that resilience is not about asking students and educators to endure hardship in silence, nor is it about celebrating struggle for struggle's sake. Instead, it is about transforming conditions so that adversity becomes a catalyst for growth rather than a barrier to opportunity. Urban education demands this level of clarity.

In districts like Youngstown, educators are called to do more than deliver curriculum. They are asked to lead, to heal, to stabilize, and to believe—often in the face of generational trauma, economic instability, staffing shortages, and shifting policy demands. Dr. Freeman names these realities honestly, without deficit framing. He situates resilience within the broader context of systems change, emphasizing that sustainable improvement requires intentional alignment of culture, leadership, instruction, and well-being.

What distinguishes Dr. Freeman's contribution is his insistence that resilience must be embedded into the fabric of school improvement efforts. His work challenges leaders to move beyond compliance-driven reform and toward coherent systems that prioritize psychological safety, professional competence, meaningful relationships, and shared purpose. This perspective aligns deeply with continuous improvement models and with the work of districts committed to long-term transformation rather than short-term fixes.

As Superintendent, I have seen firsthand that when resilience is treated as a system-level priority, outcomes change. Educators are more likely to remain in the profession. School leaders are better equipped to navigate complexity. Students experience greater consistency, trust, and opportunity. Dr. Freeman provides the field with a framework that validates these truths while offering practical strategies for implementation across diverse educational contexts.

This book also reflects a deep understanding of leadership. Dr. Freeman recognizes that educator resilience is inseparable from leadership practice. Principals and district leaders do not merely manage systems; they shape the emotional and relational climate in which teaching and learning occurs. His emphasis on purpose, connection, competence, and well-being speaks directly to the kind of leadership required to transform urban schools into places of stability, hope, and high expectation.

I am particularly honored that this book is dedicated to the educators, students, and families of the Youngstown City School District. Their resilience is not theoretical. It is lived daily in classrooms, hallways, and communities striving for renewal.

My hope is that this book serves as both a guide and a call to action. A guide for educators seeking to better support students facing adversity. A call to action for leaders and policymakers to build systems worthy of the people they serve. Dr. Freeman has given the field a work that is intellectually sound, deeply human, and urgently relevant.

When resilience is understood as a shared responsibility and embedded within systems, schools do more than improve; they transform. And in urban education, transformation is not optional. It is imperative."

By Jeremy J. Batchelor, M.S. Ed., ePHCLE, pHCLE
Superintendent, Youngstown City School District

There are certain people whose presence immediately puts others at ease—people whose work is not defined by a title, but by the way they consistently show up for others. Dr. Martin Freeman is one of those people. First and foremost, he is a genuinely good human being. His insight, compassion, and unwavering commitment to people's well-being have made him a trusted advocate for families, staff, and students throughout the Youngstown City School District.

In his role as Ombudsman, Dr. Freeman serves as a vital bridge between families, educators, and the school system. Before this role, his work as the McKinney-Vento Liaison reflected the very heart of service—ensuring that our most vulnerable students had access to necessities, dignity, and stability while helping families navigate incredibly difficult circumstances. His work has always centered on care, advocacy, and equity, and that commitment continues to define his leadership today.

Anyone who knows Dr. Freeman knows that his professionalism is matched by his humanity. When he walks into a school, he does not rush past people; he greets them. He stops. He listens. He checks in—not because he has to, but because he genuinely cares. At Rayen Early College Middle School, his visits are always welcome. He makes it a point to say hello to everyone in the main office and to any staff member or student he encounters along the way. His cheerful greetings and sincere concern leave people feeling seen and valued. And if you know him well, you also know his love for Cleveland sports—a passion he eagerly shares, often calling my husband for animated conversations that reflect his joy in connection just as much as the game itself.

Chapter 8, *Educator Resilience: The Heartbeat of a Thriving School*, speaks powerfully to the lived reality of educators in the Youngstown City School District. Teaching here—like in many urban districts—requires far more than content knowledge. It demands emotional strength, adaptability, compassion, and a deep sense of purpose. Our educators carry academic expectations while also supporting students through trauma, uncertainty, and challenges that extend beyond the classroom walls. This chapter affirms what we know to be true: resilience is not about perfection or endurance alone; it is about sustaining hope, purpose, and connection in the midst of complexity.

FACING AND OVERCOMING ADVERSITY

Doc's book puts emphasis on purpose, competence, connection, and well-being mirrors what I see daily in our schools. Purpose anchors our educators to their "why"—the belief that their work matters and that every child deserves opportunity. Competence gives them the confidence to adapt and respond to ever-changing needs. Connection sustains them through collaboration, shared problem-solving, and supportive leadership. And well-being reminds us that caring for educators is not optional; it is essential if we expect them to care for others.

In Youngstown City Schools, we proudly call our students **scholars**. That word is intentional. It reflects what we believe about our students and what we see in them every day. I believe deeply in our scholars—their brilliance, their resilience, and their capacity for success. I witness countless successes: scholars achieving academic milestones, discovering their voices, setting goals for the future, and overcoming obstacles with determination and pride. These moments of success are fueled by resilient educators who create environments where scholars feel safe, supported, challenged, and inspired.

This chapter reminds us that when educators are supported, students thrive. Resilient educators model perseverance, emotional regulation, and hope—skills our scholars absorb and carry with them. In a district like Youngstown, resilience is not an abstract concept; it is a shared practice and a collective strength. It lives in our classrooms, our relationships, and our unwavering commitment to our scholars' success.

Dr. Freeman's leadership embodies the very principles outlined in this book. His advocacy, compassion, and steady presence reinforce the systems and relationships that allow resilience to flourish. He reminds us that schools succeed not only through policies and programs, but through people—people who care deeply, lead with integrity, and believe in the promise of every child.

This work is a testament to the power of resilience, community, and belief. It honors the educators who continue to show up, the scholars who continue to strive, and the leaders—like Dr. Martin Freeman—who ensure that humanity remains at the center of education.

Dr. Maureen E. Donofrio, Ed. D.
Principal
Youngstown Rayen Early College Middle School
Youngstown City School District

"As the director of Choffin Career and Technical Center in Youngstown, Ohio. I have spent the last nine years leading a school that serves students who often carry significant adversity, including economic hardship, family instability, trauma, and the lingering effects of a global pandemic. Before coming to Youngstown, I served five years in urban education as a high school administrator in Rockford, Illinois. Across both communities, I have witnessed firsthand how resilience is not an abstract ideal but a necessity for our students, our educators, and ourselves.

At Choffin, we have built a strong culture around three very clear goals: graduate on time, earn industry certifications, and be career and college ready. These goals are more than metrics on a school report card, they are lifelines of opportunity for our students. Through our many internal initiatives for success including built in milestone achievements, our expanded support for academics with a lens in CTE, pre-apprenticeships and career placements, and a data tracking system that enables

FACING AND OVERCOMING ADVERSITY

us to create individualized success plans for each of our students, we remove barriers and open up multiple pathways to graduation and lifelong success. These efforts have allowed our students to earn a high school diploma at our school at a much higher rate than other buildings in our district and the highest among all urban career and technical centers in Ohio.

We have earned a five-star rating on the Ohio Report Card for two consecutive years and remain on track for a third year. None of this would be possible without resilient educators, administrators, and support staff who show up every day ready to guide, mentor, and believe in our students. This book speaks directly to the reality we live at Choffin, and chapter 8 especially resonates, as it articulates what I witness daily; resilient staff remaining calm in chaos, having hope in uncertainty, and perseverance through setbacks. When our staff are grounded in purpose, supported by connection, confident in their competence, and intentional in their work, they create the stable environments our students need to thrive and succeed.

This work is forged on the front lines and is dedicated to the administrators, educators, support staff, students, and families of the Youngstown City School District and the districts that resemble us. To my fellow urban school leaders and staff: this book offers a practical, evidence-informed framework to build resilience in both our students and ourselves. Read it, share it with your teams, and put its strategies into action. Our young people are counting on us. It is an honor and privilege to introduce this essential book."

MARTIN FREEMAN

Dr. Michael Saville, Ed.D.
Director
Choffin Career and Technical Center
Youngstown City School District

As I reflect on the chapters in this book, I can say that as a teacher it is an opportunity to reward them for their resiliency and understand that what they do on a daily basis is not easy and not to be taken for granted. This book reminds me of the strength, love and determination that teachers display every day as they enter into a classroom and leave the building for the day. This book reminds me of what it means to face adversity and bounce back. It reminds me of how teachers work with their students and together they face trauma, challenges and stress but they use their inner strength to overcome these barriers.

I wish I had this book when I was teaching as it would have provided me with what Dr. Martin Freeman references throughout the book on how resilience emerges at the intersection of purpose, competence, connection and well-being. It shows us the reasons we do what we do and why it is important to stay steadfast regardless of what comes our way as an educator. It shows us that resiliency is what builds our confidence within ourselves so we can be better for our students in the classroom. As you continue to read this book, you will also learn the importance of connection and the importance of one's well-being is self-care and self-reflection.

I wish I had this book when I started as an administrator because it would have provided me a clearer understanding on what it means to be resilient and what to look for in teachers. As an administrator, you too want to be resilient but you also want to have the tools to identify resilience among others. Dr.

FACING AND OVERCOMING ADVERSITY

Freeman gives you these tools with the understanding that "resilience is not simply what helps us survive: it's what teaches us how to live fully, love deeply, and lead courageously." It is the capacity to withstand and recover. Resiliency is the importance of surviving, taking a stand and believing in yourself and others. In this book, Dr. Freeman provides you with a better understanding of resilience and how to practice it throughout the classroom. As a teacher it provides you the tools needed to maintain your own resilience and also build the resiliency of our students. It is a great read that will demonstrate for educators how to cope and through these coping strategies how it will affect our students. Afterall, isn't the goal to produce resilient students?

I know Dr Freeman to be a man of great character and an upstanding leader. He not only researches but he shares real life experiences that support his writings such as building resilient teachers and students. Dr. Freeman's passion shows in this book. His experience as a social worker, pastor, and educator grants him the confidence to speak first hand on what resilient teachers look like in a school district and the power in their words and actions to bring resiliency among students. This book captures the authors' insight and provides each of you with both guidance, direction and inspiration.

Kelly D. Washington, Ph.D.
Principal/Adjunct Professor
Taft Elementary
Youngstown City School District

PREFACE

Have you ever been in a dark place? You were down for the count, Isolated, no hope. You conceptualized, internalized, even verbalized the failure, crisis, adversity you were going through? You were dismayed and couldn't see beyond what you were experiencing but with time, in time you, and through time you began to heal, bounce back, and recover. That's the reality for many children navigating adversity.

In every classroom, hallway, playground, and office, there are stories of students who wake up each day carrying more than backpacks. Many come with grief, instability, trauma, pressure, and invisible battles that shape how they learn, behave, and see their future. Yet, time and again, we also see something powerful emerge—students who discover strength, connection, and hope even in the midst of challenge. This book, Facing and Overcoming Adversity: A Strategic Approach to Building K–12 Resilient Students, was written for the educators, leaders, and caring adults who believe that resilience is not accidental; that it can be nurtured, taught, and strengthened with intentional practice.

Trauma, struggle, setbacks, disappointment, failure, challenge, and grief are all part of the human experience but so is resilience. Many of our children have experienced, are experiencing, or will experience feeling down and out, depressed, dejected, defeated? Many of them, unable to verbalize are internally asking themselves, when will the hurt, pain, and suffering end? How much longer do I have to endure the misery, and the suffocating thoughts that render me discouraged, even disconnected? They ask themselves, can I, will I get through this dark time in my life?

Resilience is not about eliminating hardship; it is about equipping students with the inner resources, external support, and learning environments that help them adapt, heal, and thrive. Schools are uniquely positioned to do this work. They are more than academic institutions—they are centers of belonging, safety, restoration, and human growth. This book provides a practical, research-informed roadmap to help school communities cultivate resilience in purposeful, compassionate, and strategic ways.

Resilience isn't just about "bouncing back," it's significant in that it's about growing through challenges, developing emotional strength, and learning that setbacks don't define us. Resilience, for children, develop throughout their lives and is attained by what they observe and imitate. It's built through relationships, support, and the environments we create for them, especially educators.

We tend to idealize childhood as a carefree time, but youth alone doesn't offer a shield against the emotional hurts, challenges, and trauma many of our children face. Our children are asked to deal with problems ranging from adapting to a new classroom, online schooling, struggles at home and deadly encounters in their neighborhoods, communities, and city streets. Also, they face the uncertainties that are part of growing up in a complex world. How many of you reading this book know that childhood can be anything but carefree? The ability to thrive despite these challenges arises from the skills of learning to be resilient. Make no mistake, ups and downs, changes and turnarounds are part of life but in the long run, those challenges can help our children become stronger and teach them valuable lessons.

In this book we're going to explore how we, as an educational system can foster resilience, helping children not just survive adversity but thrive regardless of it. I'm confident the strategies provided will unlock resilience in ways that will engage you, allowing you to glean and grasp from these strategies, then teaching and helping our children practically apply them to their lives.

My hope is that these pages affirm what educators already know in their hearts: that every student has capacity, potential, and worth—and with the right systems, relationships, and supports, they can rise beyond adversity and build lives anchored in strength, hope, and possibility.

FACING AND OVERCOMING ADVERSITY

INTRODUCTION

Every day, in classrooms, hallways, and homes across our communities, students are fighting battles we cannot always see. Some carry the weight of fractured families, silent trauma, unmet needs, academic pressure, or environments that challenge their sense of safety and belonging. Despite these obstacles something remarkable continues to rise within them: It's called resilience.

Resilience is not the absence of hardship; it is the courage to stand in the midst of it. It is the quiet determination of a student who shows up to school even when life looks bleak, and they feel overwhelmed. It is the strength of a student who refuses to let failure define them. It is the hope that emerges in young people who choose growth instead of giving up.

Students are not shaped by the adversity itself, but by the support, skills, and belief systems that help them push through it. Resilience grows when caring adults' (parents, guardians, teachers, social workers, coaches) step in, when schools create safe spaces, and when students learn that their story is not limited by their struggle, and in fact, has yet to be told. What they face may challenge them but it doesn't and must not defeat them.

This generation of students today, must rise above circumstances that often breaks others. When we teach them how to harness resilience, we're not just helping them survive difficult moments we're empowering them to transform adversity into strength, struggle into wisdom, and obstacles into opportunities. Their resilience is not just a skill; it is their gateway to hope, healing, and a future filled with possibility.

Resilience is not born in the peaceful setting of tranquility, but forged in the fires of adversity. It's in the struggle, not the stillness, that strength takes place—it is discovered in the storms of life. It does not call out its presence; it discloses itself through the moments when we choose to rise again, when we encourage ourselves to get up one more time. Resilience is the human spirit's declaration that I've been broken but not defeated, and weary does not mean I'm done.

In classrooms, communities, and homes, we see resilience every day. It's the teacher who shows up for students after facing their own losses. It's the student who keeps believing that tomorrow can be better than today. It's the parent who chooses to love their child with hope, even when life feels uncertain.

This book is about that kind of strength—the kind that grows quietly beneath the surface. It's about how adversity can become the soil where purpose takes root, how hope can be practiced, and how healing can become a way of life.

Resilience is not simply what helps us survive; it's what teaches us how to live fully, love deeply, and lead courageously. Resilience teaches us that adversity does not define us—it develops us. It reveals that strength is often born out of struggle and that setbacks, while painful, can become powerful turning points. Through resilience, we learn that we are far more capable than we ever imagined, that asking for help is an act of courage, and that hope can carry us through even the darkest seasons. Resilience shows us how to adapt when life shifts, how to regulate our emotions when they feel overwhelming, and how to hold on to purpose when challenges try to distract us. Most of all, resilience reminds us that healing is possible—that our past may shape us, but it does not have to limit our future.

My hope is that as you turn these pages, you'll not only learn about resilience but you'll begin to see it in yourself.

Chapter 1 – The Meaning of Resilience

When tackling this question what is resilience, I knew from the onset it would be a daunting challenge. The field of resilience research is not short on inquiry, and defining resilience comes with a plethora of explanations. When discussing resilience, one must consider

(1) how should resilience be defined,

(2) what are the critical factors of resilience,

(3) how does the science of resilience inform research today,

(4) and how can we practically apply resilience to everyday living.

Those in the field of research today stand on the shoulders of giants, meaning those who've trod the path of discovery and who worked tirelessly to provide a framework that sill helps us grasp the very meaning of the term resilience today. Norman Germezy, Emmy Werner, Michael Rutter, and Ann Masten (still living) were and are the pioneers of resilience research. Their work focused on understanding how children coped with adversity and were able to thrive despite their difficult circumstances.

I trust that, reading this book, you will agree that resilience is an intricate word that can be defined differently in the context of individuals, families, organizations, societies, and cultures. The research and science of resilience continues to build as now fields of neuroscience, mental health, medicine, psychology, and sociology have emerged and engaged in the quest to bring understanding to this word.

The word resilient is the new "buzz," word today. Resilience is a word being used across disciplines, sectors and professions. You will hear the word used in politics, sports, even in the halls of academia. Though it is a word frequently being used, it is often used out of context. When asked what resilience means, the answer varies from vague to often misunderstood, depending on who you ask, and in what setting it is being used.

Psychologist, from the 1970's, until present day have defined resilience in various ways: Garmezy defined resilience as, "Not necessarily impervious to stress. Rather, resilience is designed to reflect the capacity for recovery and maintained adaptive behavior that may follow initial retreat or incapacity upon initiating a stressful event" (Garmezy, 1991a).

Masten defined resilience as, "The capacity of a dynamic system to adapt successfully to disturbances that threaten system function, viability, or future development of the system" (Ann Masten, 2014).

Rutter defined resilience as, "An interactive concept that is concerned with the combination of serious risk experiences and a relatively positive psychological outcome despite those experiences" (Rutter, 2006).

Werner defined resilience as, "The capacity [of individuals] to cope effectively with the internal stresses of their vulnerabilities (labile patterns of autonomic reactivity, developmental imbalances, unusual sensitivities) and external stresses (illness, major losses, and dissolution of the family)" (Werner, 1982).

Many others have contributed definitions and explanations of resilience however, the most clear, concise, and poignant definition of resilience, in my opinion, is "The ability to weather and recover from adversity" (Southwick et al. 2014). The aforementioned definition is simple, yet profound.

We must recognize that adversity is multifaceted and in that, regarding children we could include child abuse, exposure to neighborhood violence, even family economic hardships (Bethel et al. 2014). Children's ability to weather (navigate) through the many obstacles that they will face requires them to find strength in vulnerability, and to work through those obstacles in spite of the potential outcomes. I strongly believe this is "weathering and recovering," at its best.

Building and fostering resilience in children, in times of adversity, is necessary more than ever because of the times we're living in today. It doesn't matter a child's race, color or creed; their socioeconomic position, neighborhood background, or family origin, resilience is necessary.

Identifying and understanding resilience is critical for every child. I'm a realist so I realize resilience won't stop problems from arising, neither magically cause them to disappear however, having resilience will help children see beyond their problems, and find answers to enjoy life without being overcome with stress.

Key Considerations Concerning Resilience

Resilience is born out of, forged through, and developed through adversity.

When a child experiences adversity his or her strength to overcome becomes a building block of DNA. The ability for children to adapt, persevere, and grow increases exponentially as they face and deal with adversity. It's in moments of trouble, hardship, and crisis that a child must determine to adjust and push forward regardless of the hurt, pain, and suffering. When a child learns to look adversity in the face and be resolute to continue pushing forward is when resilience shines so bright.

Resilience is a process that develops with time

How children deal with trauma, stress, and adversity takes time. We may not see the effects of what has happened to children but as they matriculate though life, from birthday to birthday, from grade to grade, and through various relationships we will have a better idea as to the impact the aforementioned events will have on their lives.

Experiencing distress does not diminish a child's resilience

Although depression, anxiety, and stress may be symptomatic of adverse experiences, it should not lead onlookers to believe a child is not resilient. Children can be dealing with everyday challenges such as family issues, challenges in school, and peer problems all while still being resilient.

Overcoming challenges through resilience often lead to personal growth

A high school student once told me that working through setbacks in life helped create a sense of urgency to keep pushing ahead, and pursuing a path that would lead to college. This student, as result of adversity, gained an increased sense of meaning as they dealt with, and continued forward in spite of the adversity experienced. We must never underestimate how setbacks, challenges, and trials can help students grasp a more significant motivation to work through, around, even during tumultuous times.

The way resilience manifest can change at different stages of life

Dr. Bhatnager says, "One way of thinking or acting might be more helpful at one point in someone's life, but not at another. Think about a child who has no one to turn to in their life – they need to be self-sufficient and scrappy to survive and thrive. But when they get older and have more people around them who care for them, reaching out and asking for help in tough times would be a marker of personal resilience." (Bhatnager, 2002)

Resilience is shaped by the environment and circumstances

The focus here means that resilience is not just an internal trait but is influenced by a person's environment, relationships, culture, and circumstances. The ability to adapt and recover from challenges depends on factors such as support systems, access to resources, and past experiences.

A student's resilience in school may depend on supportive teachers, a safe learning environment, and personal coping strategies. Similarly, a student facing trauma may demonstrate resilience differently based on their social connections and community resources.

Why my pursuit with identifying and understanding resilience?

While attending and presenting at a conference (Innovative Schools Summit) in Orlando, Florida I heard a question asked of a presenter concerning trauma. The question was asked how does resilience play a role in children working through trauma. This question not only captured my attention but has fueled me to pursue the essence of resilience as it relates to its impact on children in school facing adverse situations, circumstances, even conditions. I further sought to correlate how building resilience in schools is critical in this day and time.

Resilience is adapting and recovering in the face of challenges. Children won't and can't avoid hardships therefore, it is crucial for them to learn to develop the capacity to navigate difficulties with perseverance and hope. For children in school, resilience plays a critical role in their emotional well-being, academic success, and social development.

Resilience is key in many areas academically for example:

<u>Emotional regulation</u> – resilient students learn to manage difficulty, disappointment, and overcome fear and doubt.

<u>Academic performance</u> - resilient students are better prepared to work through test anxiety, curriculum changes, and unexpected changes.

<u>Social relationships</u> - resilient students have better relationships with peers, and can work towards solving conflicts with peers, and seek adult support when needed.

<u>Behavioral adaptability</u> - resilient students use coping skills to overcome problems related to home, deal with transitions, and manage expectations without being overwhelmed.

<u>Sustained achievement</u> – resilient children, via weathering and recovering from adversity, are equipped with skills that allow them to navigate challenging experiences, learn from setbacks, and drive through adverse situations, which ultimately lead to sustained academic success.

Also, educational practitioners have long played and continue to play a pivotal role in fostering resilience by creating supportive environments in their classrooms, implementing and practically applying restorative practices, and teaching applicable coping skills. Trauma-informed approaches, strong teacher-student relationships, and access to mental health resources can all contribute to a school and climate that nurtures resilience.

As I move to conclude this chapter let me share that Resilience in education is not developed on calm days when every student is engaged, every lesson flows perfectly, and every parent's email ends

FACING AND OVERCOMING ADVERSITY

with gratitude. It is forged in the unpredictable moments when technology fails, when a student shuts down emotionally, and when behavior erupts unexpectedly, or when your lesson plan doesn't' flow as planned. Resilience manifests when your heart is tired, the data feels discouraging, and yet you still show up and your mind is ready, heart open, determined to try again.

Educators don't just teach resilience; they live it. They model it every time they adapt, rethink, support, or start over. Resilience in the classroom is not about perfection, it's about persistence. It's not about having all the answers, it's about believing there is still a solution worth finding.

Resilience is the quiet strength behind every teaching practitioner who says, "Today was hard. Tomorrow, I'll try again; better, wiser, stronger." It is the fuel of hope, the anchor of purpose, and the heartbeat of every classroom where growth is more important than perfection.

Chapter 2 – Why the Science of Resilience Matters

The science of resilience explores how people, especially children and adults in demanding contexts, adapt, recover, and grow despite stress, adversity, and trauma. Its importance lies in several key areas that we will address.

Instead of defining individuals by problems or risk factors, resilience research helps us see the protective factors such as supportive relationships, coping skills, hope, purpose, and environments that heal rather than harm.

The science of resilience shows that the brain is elastic, skills like emotional regulation, problem-solving, and stress management can be developed. This means resilience isn't a personality trait but teachable and buildable.

Resilience calls attention to conditions that help people thrive. In other words, resilience is manifested in safe relationships, equitable environments, predictable structure, and communities that cultivate belonging. Schools, health systems, and workplaces can design policies and cultures that buffer stress and promote well-being. Research shows resilience supports mental health, improves academic and life outcomes, reduces risk behaviors, and strengthens emotional and physical well-being across the lifespan.

Resilience science provides a narrative of possibility. It should be noted that adversity does not define destiny. When the right supports and skills are in place, people can recover, grow, and often become stronger and more compassionate because of what they've overcome.

I am convinced that resilience science equips teachers to respond with compassion, trauma-awareness, restorative practices, and strategies that build competence, connection, and confidence.

Practical Application of Resilience Science in K–12 Education: An Evidence-Based Perspective

Resilience in children and adolescents is not merely an individual trait; it is a dynamic, interactional process shaped by biology, relationships, environment, and opportunities for growth (Masten, 2014). The science of resilience demonstrates that the brain is highly responsive to context. Supportive environments, strong relationships, predictable structures, and intentional skill-building can significantly strengthen a student's capacity to adapt and thrive despite adversity (National Scientific Council on the Developing Child, 2015).

Understanding these scientific foundations allows educators to intentionally create classroom environments and school systems that buffer stress, support regulation, and promote optimal learning and development.

Resilience Depends on Safety and Regulation

The ability to learn, think clearly, and behave appropriately is deeply connected to the functioning of the stress-response system. When students experience prolonged or intense stress without adequate support, the body shifts into a state of survival, reducing capacity for attention, memory, reasoning, and behavioral control (Perry & Szalavitz, 2006).

Implication for Classrooms

Emotionally safe and predictable environments reduce hyperarousal and allow higher-order thinking to occur. Classroom practices such as calm adult responses, consistent structure, relational tone, and non-shaming discipline contribute to regulation and improved learning outcomes (Bath, 2008; Brunzell, Stokes, & Waters, 2016).

Relationships Are the Primary Protective Factor

A consistent research finding is that the strongest predictor of resilience in youth is the presence of at least one stable, nurturing, and supportive adult relationship (Masten, 2001). Relationships buffer stress, promote neural regulation, and communicate worth and belonging (National Scientific Council on the Developing Child, 2015).

Implication for Schools

Intentional relationship-building practices such as personal check-ins, positive teacher-student interactions, mentoring structures, and restorative approaches—enhance resilience while also reducing behavioral incidents and improving engagement (Furlong, O'Brennan, & You, 2011).

Resilience Requires Explicit Skill-Building

Resilient students are not simply "naturally strong"; they are equipped with emotional, cognitive, and social skills developed over time. These include emotional awareness, self-regulation, problem-solving, communication, perseverance, and adaptive thinking (Compas et al., 2017).

Implication for Instruction

Schools enhance resilience when they integrate:
- Social-emotional learning instruction
- Emotional literacy development

- Explicit regulation strategies (breathing, grounding, reflection)
- Opportunities for students to practice coping and problem-solving

Evidence supports that SEL programming leads to improved academic outcomes, reduced behavioral concerns, and better long-term well-being (Durlak et al., 2011).

Meaning, Purpose, and Agency Strengthen Resilience

Students are more likely to persist through difficulty when they perceive their lives and learning as meaningful. Purpose fosters psychological endurance and strengthens motivation (Snyder, 2002). Agency is the belief that one's actions can influence outcomes—and directly supports resilience (Zimmerman, 2002; Ungar, 2015).

Implication for Educators

Classrooms that provide:

- Choice
- Leadership opportunities
- Voice in decision-making

Opportunities to see personal competence and progress create environments that cultivate ownership, dignity, and resilience (Bandura, 1997).

Normalize Struggle as Part of Learning

Research on growth mindset demonstrates that when students view intelligence and ability as malleable rather than fixed, they approach challenges with greater persistence and emotional resilience (Dweck, 2006, p. 215). Likewise, academic resilience is built when struggle is framed as a normal, expected, and valuable part of learning rather than as failure.

Implication for Classrooms

Feedback that emphasizes effort, strategy, and progress rather than innate ability promotes resilience and long-term achievement (Hattie & Timperley, 2007).

Predictability and Structure Reduce Anxiety

Predictable routines and consistent expectations reduce uncertainty, which in turn lowers stress responses and supports cognitive functioning (Shonkoff et al., 2012). Structure does not restrict growth; it creates the safety needed for growth to occur.

Implication for School Practice

Reliable daily schedules, consistent expectations, clear communication, and emotionally stable environments contribute directly to stronger behavior regulation and improved readiness to learn (Bath, 2008).

Adult Resilience Matters

The regulation capacity of adults significantly affects student outcomes. Dysregulated adults unintentionally escalate student dysregulation, while calm, emotionally regulated educators support neural regulation in children (Perry & Szalavitz, 2017). Teacher well-being is therefore both an ethical responsibility and an instructional strategy.

Implication for Schools

Systems that support educator mental health, collegial support, reflective practice, and emotional sustainability produce stronger student resilience and healthier learning environments (Jennings & Greenberg, 2009).

In conclusion, when science and resilience are joined, we move beyond inspirational language and enter a space of intentional, evidence-informed practice. Science helps us understand how resilient systems are built, why certain students thrive despite adversity, and what conditions best nurture strength, healing, and hope. Neuroscience reminds us that the brain is adaptable; it can learn, heal, and rewire through experience, supportive relationships, and consistent emotional safety. Psychology and resilience research demonstrate that skills like self-regulation, meaning-making, cognitive flexibility, and connection are not accidental traits—they can be taught, strengthened, and sustained. Educational science shows that classrooms grounded in belonging, relevance, high expectations, and relational trust create learning environments where resilience naturally grows.

When science informs resilience, we do not simply wish students to be strong—we intentionally cultivate it. We design schools where emotional well-being is not separate from academic success, but a necessary foundation for it. We empower teachers with strategies grounded in research rather than exhaustion. And we build educational communities where resilience becomes a predictable outcome, not a fortunate accident. Science gives resilience credibility, structure, and direction; resilience gives science heart, humanity, and purpose. Joined together, they create the conditions where both teachers and students can thrive, even in the face of adversity.

Chapter 3 – The Nature and Nurture of Resilience

Resilience is one of my favorite things to write about because it represents not only one of my core values but also one of my greatest strengths. It's also the defining characteristic of the work I have the privilege of doing in public education.

I'm convinced that I've always been a resilient person, mostly because, my upbringing demanded me to be so. When things fell apart, I didn't have the luxury of time to wallow, wait or throw a pity-party. When plans failed, I looked to other plans and kept moving forward. In other words, I was resourceful. I wondered if I was predisposed to "weathering and recovering from adversity?" I believe my ability to be resilient came from my wonderful and resilient mother. I learned so much from watching her, and other mentors turn adversity into action with determination.

The debate over whether resilience is based on nature or nurture has been ongoing for decades. Both sides make compelling arguments, suggesting that resilience isn't one or the other but a dynamic interplay between genetic makeup and environmental influence. From a nature perspective, some people appear naturally more resilient due to genetic factors. From a nurture perspective, resilience is shaped by experiences, relationships, and environments.

Supportive relationships, positive role models, and exposure to manageable challenges help build strong coping skills. Secure attachment in early childhood, encouragement, meaningful responsibilities, and even cultural values all contribute to strengthening resilience over time. Schools, communities, and life experiences play a powerful role in cultivating it. So, can anyone become resilient? Research increasingly supports the answer of yes

While genetics may set the stage, resilience is not a fixed trait but a capacity that can be developed, strengthened, and trained. Skills such as emotional regulation, mindfulness, hopefulness, problem-solving, and stress management can all enhance resilience. Building strong social connections, maintaining a growth mindset, practicing gratitude, and learning from setbacks also help individuals recover and thrive.

Understanding resilience as a blend of nature and nurture allows us to move beyond the question of whether we are resilient to the more pertinent question of how we can become more resilient. While some may have a natural predisposition, anyone regardless of background, history, or genetics—can build, strengthen, and sustain resilience through intentional practice, supportive relationships, and environments that nurture growth.

In chapter 1 we shared that resilience was, "weathering and recovering from adversity." It simply means adapting and thriving. This has fascinated psychologists, educators, and researchers for many years. The question is asked why do some individuals recover quickly from hardships while others struggle? This question has fueled the age-old nature versus nurture debate, which seeks to determine whether resilience is primarily a product of genetic inheritance or shaped by life experiences. Many argue that resilience is hardwired into our DNA but again there is no such thing as a resilience gene. Others emphasize the critical role of supportive environments, early childhood experiences, and learned coping mechanisms. I purport the proposition that nature and nurture work together to shape human adaptability and strength.

Resilience in children is not an accident. It is neither fully inherited nor entirely taught but is shaped by both nature and nurture, working together like two hands that mold and strengthen a child's capacity to adapt, cope, and grow through challenges. When talking about whether resilience is nurture vs nature many factors play a significant role. The role of genetics (nature) is unquestionably important. There are biological factors. Such as efficient stress response systems, neural circuitry, immune responses, and epigenetic changes, all influenced by genetics and environmental factors. There are neurological factors such as the ability of the brain to adapt and recover from trauma, stress, and adversity. Also, neural circuits, brain structure, and stress hormones play a significant role.

Let's look at nature as the inner wiring of resilience. Some children seem naturally more adaptable, optimistic, or emotionally steady. These traits are not just personality as they are influenced by genetics, temperament, and brain development. From birth, children possess differing levels of temperament, emotional regulation, and stress control.

First, consider temperament. Some students are naturally more easygoing or flexible, while others are sensitive, intense, or cautious. A student in your classroom may be one who nothing seems to incite a rash emotional response about anything. Another student in your classroom is enraged by the slightest joke, insult, or negative gesture from a peer. Be mindful that a child's temperament can affect how they handle frustration, change, and conflict.

Second, consider emotional regulation capacity. The brain's prefrontal cortex (responsible for decision-making, impulse control, and emotional balance) develops at different rates in children. Therefore, some students may be more naturally equipped to pause, reflect, and calm themselves before reacting. For example: Dennis, a fifth grader, is being laughed at because his peers saw his mother kiss him at drop-off. Dennis chuckles and says, "You guys are so immature." Dennis is able to pause, reflect, and stay calm as he delineates his classmate's behavior towards him.

Third, consider the stress response system. Students have different biological responses to stress. Some recover quickly from setbacks, while others feel overwhelmed for longer periods of time. This is linked to genetics, brain chemistry, and early experiences. Nature gives each student a unique starting point, but it does not determine their finish line. This is where nurture plays a critical role.

Then there's the role of environment or (nurture). The way a student develops helps define how resilient they will become. How secure is the student's attachments? We must consider how supportive the parents are as well as how the child engages in school, relationships, and extra-curricular activities. Is there reinforcement that is positive on part of teachers, community leaders, even family?

I believe both nature and nurture are important. Genetics play a role in the beginning stages of shaping how a child will handle adversity. The environment plays a role in how resilience continues to develop over the life span. I strongly support genetics (nature) however, environment (nurture) a child's life experiences, social support, and learned coping skills play a more significant role in shaping the child's ability to weather and recover from the trials of life.

Think of nature as a student who is anxious, then nurture as a teacher providing predictable routines for the student. Think of nature as an impulsive student, then nurture as a teacher who provides clear boundaries for the student. Think of nature as an introverted student, then nurture as a teacher who uses reflective activities and encouragement for the student. Finally, think of nature as an easily discouraged student, then nurture as a teacher who uses resilient language.

Resilience is not built when barriers are removed. It is a process where students are supported enough to try, allowed to fail, and encouraged to persist. Students need scaffolded challenges. In other words, challenges, tasks, problems difficult enough to cause them to stretch but supported enough to help them through the process.

This discourse on whether resilience is rooted in nature or nurture reveals that it is best understood through a biopsychosocial lens. **Genetic predispositions may shape an individual's baseline capacity** for stress regulation and emotional adaptability, yet environmental contexts, including secure relationships, cultural influences, and lived experiences, play a critical role in the development and strengthening of resilient behaviors. Rather than a static trait, resilience emerges as a dynamic, malleable process influenced by both inherited factors and intentional cultivation. This understanding underscores the importance of designing supportive environments, policies, and interventions that promote resilience across diverse populations, irrespective of individual starting points.

To end this chapter, I would like to share a familiar story about "Two Seeds." Two seeds were planted on the same day, but in very different places. The first seed fell on rich soil beside a quiet river. It was surrounded by warmth, steady sunlight, and gentle rain. Its roots grew easily, pushing into soft earth, drawing nourishment without struggle. Everything around it supported its growth. This seed represented nurture—a supportive environment that builds resilience through stability, encouragement, and protection.

The second seed landed in rocky ground on the side of a windy hill. The soil was thin, water was scarce, and every day it faced the force of harsh winds. Its roots had to fight for depth, anchoring around stones and cracks. It grew slowly, bending and stretching toward whatever light it could find. Day after day it endured what other seeds never had to face. This seed represented nature—the innate drive to survive, adapt, and push forward even when resources are limited.

As the years passed, both seeds became trees—but they were not the same. The tree by the river grew tall and straight, supported by the steady environment that nurtured it. The tree on the hill grew shorter and more rugged, its trunk thicker, its roots deeper than anyone imagined. It had weathered storms the other tree never knew. Though shaped by hardship, it had developed a strength and stability uniquely its own.

Both trees were resilient—but their resilience came from different sources. The river tree's resilience was built through nurture—consistent support, a safe environment, and the steady presence of what it needed. The hill tree's resilience was shaped by nature—innate grit, adaptation, and the ability to grow through pressure.

Together, their story shows a powerful truth - Resilience is not formed in only one way. Some students develop it because they were nurtured well. Others develop it because life forced them to. And many grow resilient through a blend of both - innate strength supported by caring adults who help them flourish.

Chapter 4 – Why Is Resilience Important

The importance of resilience in school-aged children, from my perspective, should not be overestimated. In times of despair, desperation, and doubt resilience can be the x-factor that propels a student to stay in school in spite the road that appears long and winding. When life for a child in school appears to be overwhelming and dark the resilient student can pull from their reservoir of resilience strategies to look beyond past failure, hardships, and problems their facing, ultimately looking to the future for hope that transcends adversity.

Isn't it amazing how our students can be naturally resilient? I'm always amazed watching a student's bounce back from adversity. Challenges, disappointments, and failure comes with the territory for k-12 students. It's refreshing to see students struggle academically but overcome. It's even better when students forging ahead to the next challenge to conquer, the next obstacle to negotiate, and the next lesson to learn how to weather and overcome adversity. That being said, parents, educators, mental health workers everywhere should come to embrace that resilience is an ability that children can develop and that can and will be influenced by various environmental factors. It's fact that resilience isn't a fixed trait that you simply have or don't have but a dynamic ability to conquer barriers that's supported by other protective factors and essential relational skills.

The American Psychological Association defines resilience as "the process and outcome of successfully adapting to difficult or challenging life experiences, especially through mental, emotional, and behavioral flexibility and adjustment to external and internal demands."

So, why is resilience necessary for students of all ages? When we consider research, much analysis has associated resilience to various outcomes, such as, academic success, higher connections, better stress management, and increased well-being. Students who exhibit resilience were determined to report greater levels of school involvement, and task focused.

When we consider the context of social skills enhancement, resilience is distinct because it isn't an independent ability or result like emotion management, self-awareness, relationship-building, or problem-solving. While similar, it's more exact to think of resilience as a potential constructed on the foundation of the aforementioned proficiencies. Resilience, though many definitions have been communicated, and it has various components, doesn't mean it isn't necessary. Many educators have come to recognize resilience as an important ability that a student should develop.

What skills can help students build the skills they need to be resilient? What follows are a number of ways social emotional learning programs can help students build the skills that manifest resilience. These skills aid students in navigating the intricacies of life in and out of school.

Resilience requires emotion management. Resilience is not stifling a student's emotions in the face of adversity. Instead, resilience arises from a student's ability to understand and manage the difficult emotions that originate in the face of adversity such as fear, frustration, anger, even sadness.

A core personal competency is Self-management, which encompasses a student's ability to manage their emotions, as well as an ingredient in building resilience. Like adults, kids experience myriads of emotions all the time, but especially when dealing with adversity.

Social emotional learning enables students to identify and manage emotions. It gives students strategies to name and understand how their emotions help them work through adversity. This knowledge and these strategies could make the difference between a student either becoming stressed and quitting when difficulties arise, and continuing to deal with the adversity and move forward.

Interpersonal skills support resilience. Resilience is an individual skill however, it is also, as much as we may think of resilience as an individualized skill, resilience is also developed on a student's ability to form and maintain healthy, supportive relationships. You have heard the saying, "When the going gets tough, the tough get going." Contrary to this adage, students who are resilient look for and rely on others for support.

The ability to build and maintain healthy relationships is a foundational personal and relational competency as well as a central focus of many classroom-based human skills programs and interventions. These programs provide students with meaningful opportunities to observe, understand, and practice healthy relationship skills in real classroom settings. This can include a wide range of skills, from managing conflict to interacting effectively with people who are different from themselves.

As children develop their ability to connect with and depend on others, they become better equipped to navigate challenging experiences. When obstacles arise, children with strong relationship skills understand that they don't have to face them alone—they have friends, family, and teachers who can support them when they fail an algebra test, don't make the soccer team, or lose someone they love.

FACING AND OVERCOMING ADVERSITY

These healthy relationship skills help them process, cope with, and work through life's difficult moments.

Responsible decision-making raises resilience. Another key to understanding resilience in children is recognizing the role of decision-making. Responsible decision-making is a core competency that includes curiosity, open-mindedness, the ability to make reasoned judgments after analyzing information, identifying solutions to personal and social problems, and anticipating the consequences of one's actions. These skills directly support a child's capacity to navigate and overcome challenges.

I will now tell you a story that will help you identify how resilience helps students, through responsible decision-making. Let me take you back in time to John Adams High School in Cleveland, Ohio. The year was 1978. I was a freshman (10th grade). I had come to the school as a touted Junior High Track & Field athlete looking to bolster the already loaded team of, and long history of phenomenal sprinters. The man I still refer to as my surrogate father, James Patterson, was coach and responsible for my development. I was coming off a good indoor season, and was poised to help the team win a State Championship. I had worked my way into being one of the top sprinters on the team, and member of the potential State Champion 4 x200 relay.

It was the custom that if another teammate wanted to challenge another relay member for a spot on the relay, he could do so by requesting what coach called a "Runoff." I was challenged of all people. I didn't believe I should have been challenged being one of the top sprinters on the team however, life came at me face that day in the Spring of 1978. Four young men (students) lined up at the 200-meter start line. The gun went off and away we went. The outcome was I finished 3rd, meaning I would not be on the 4 x 200 relay for the upcoming meet as only the top 2 joined the relay.

Defeated, deflated, and disgusted, I picked up my sweats and vacated the track saying, "I quit." I went to the locker room to gather my belongings only to encounter coach Patterson who walked in saying, "Marty, disappointments will happen, things will not always go your way." He then said something that even as I write, brings tears to my eyes, but forever changed my life. Coach said, "Marty, you have a choice. Put your sweats and shoes back on and get to the track or allow defeat to define who you are." Needless to say, I made my way back to the track and the rest is history. Moving forward, I experienced many defeats but resilience had been forged and I was better as result of the defeat that day.

Defeat and Coach Patterson's words caused me to make a decision to continue becoming resilient. I was able to "weather and recover from adversity." Responsible decision-making raised my ability to be resilient. Further, I believe every student should have the blessing of a Principal, Teacher, Coach to help them learn to "weather and recover from adversity."

Resilience, then, isn't about rigid strength or simply "pushing through" adversity. Another helpful illustration is surfing—sometimes catching the wave, sometimes missing it, and continually adjusting to the motion of the ocean around you. Similarly, children who have developed resilience are able to respond to difficulties with flexibility, think critically about their situation, and make thoughtful decisions about how to move forward.

The benefits of resilience in children are almost too many to name. Resilience helps them stay connected with others, remain motivated in school and extracurricular activities, and build confidence. It fuels

FACING AND OVERCOMING ADVERSITY

academic success, supports emotional well-being, and lays the groundwork for long-term personal and social growth.

While there's no single formula for building resilience in students, comprehensive human skills instruction in the classroom is a powerful foundation. Core competencies—such as relationship skills, emotional regulation, and responsible decision-making—equip children with the tools needed to adapt, persevere, and thrive. These strengths shape not just their school experience, but their development for years to come.

The question of resilience being important is easy for me to answer and should bring clarity as to why every student should learn, develop, and grow from adversity. When answering this question, I considered my own life as a student growing up in the inner-city of Cleveland, Ohio. The adversity experienced was palpable. My parents divorced and after the divorce, at the age of 11, I experienced growing up in a single parent home for most of my early school life. I realized quickly that divorce meant instability in the home as my mother struggled to raise four children. Adversity would come in many shapes, sizes and forms. There were times of food insecurity, utilities not paid (some of you know what that looks and feels like), and the inability of my mother to not have the finances for me to participate in extra-curricular sporting activities.

It was in the aforementioned times, that resilience continued to form. Learning how to weather and recover from adversity would become a common theme as I negotiated life minute by minute, hour by hour, day by day, week by week, month by month, and year by year. I would learn that when one door closed, I was to look for another door. A great example was at age ten, I had a best friend named Henry who live 6 houses from me. His father would ask if I could go to Niagara Falls with them. My parents said yes however, on the day of the trip my mother was unable to provide monies necessary for me to take the trip. It was in this time of disappointment that I began working a paper route to earn money so that I could engage in certain desired activities.

Life would again teach me resilience at a young age when in Junior High I thought being involved and good in sports meant I could be a slouch in the classroom. My track coach, during my 7th grade year, informed me that unless I could maintain a 2.5% grade average, I wouldn't be allowed to run track. The conversation came at the time I was carrying a 1.9% grade average. I informed my mother of the conversation with my coach and she confirmed my greatest fear. My mother, though she didn't graduate from high school, was a staunch advocate of education ultimately said, "You will not run until you arrive at your intended grade point average of 2/5%.

It was in those six weeks prior to the start of the track season that I would learn resilience. I struggled in science and math. I stayed after school with my teachers, used tutors, and worked tirelessly to achieve the goal of the required 2.5% grade average. I learned the power of resilience in those days when my friends were practicing, playing, and enjoying life.

The last example I want to share with you, as to why resilience is important, takes place in college. It was my freshman year at Kent State University. I was in college on a track & field scholarship. Because of my low-grade point average out of high school (yes, I being an extraordinary athlete caused me to again believe I didn't need to focus in class), I was put in remedial English. My instructor (I can't remember her name) was tough on me. I would turn in papers and she would return them with red ink, meaning the papers were below standard. I would often leave class frustrated, angry, even bewildered as to why my papers were sub-standard.

I decided to ask for a meeting with her. After class I had the courage (resilience) to ask for help. That day changed my life as she shared with me how to write better, learning good writing mechanics. The end of the semester would come and though I would only earn a "C" in her class it taught me the power of resilience as I would spend hours using the mechanics, strategies, and tools she provided so that I could learn to write. I'm forever indebted to my instructor for then I didn't realize I would need the skills she provided for me to become the writer I've become today.

Chapter 5 – The Foundations of Resilience

The foundation of resilience is built on key elements that allow children to adapt, recover, and grow through challenges. In this chapter I will address four main pillars that allow resilience to manifest in the lives of students.

The first pillar is **Self-awareness**: This pillar helps children respond thoughtfully rather than impulsively. Self-awareness is critical for personal growth and well-being. Self-awareness focuses on helping children understand their emotions, triggers, strengths, and limits. There are many skills we could elaborate on however, increasing self-awareness is an essential cornerstone to building emotional intelligence and resilience.

When we encourage young pliable minds to be mindful of their thoughts and self-talk is used in moments of adversity, we set the foundation for resilience. As parents, educators, and mental health practitioners, we must always dive into the power of challenging negativity, embracing positivity, and understanding emotional landscapes. We are commissioned to teach, planting seeds of self-awareness that will grow into self-discovery and emotional strength.

Increasing self-awareness is pivotal to build resilience in children. Self-awareness allows children to gain insight into their thoughts, emotions, and reactions. Being conscious of their thinking processes and self-talk in the moment helps them develop an understanding of how their minds work.

FACING AND OVERCOMING ADVERSITY

For example, think about a young boy who gets angry during a game because of losing. The child blames everyone accept him or herself. The child is unable to recognize the frustration and instead abruptly decides to disengage from the game. This interplay between recognizing and managing emotions is essential for navigating relationships, handling challenges, setting and achieving goals.

Self-awareness is a necessary component of helping students understand who they are (strengths, needs, and emotions), how they feel (emotional identification), why they feel the way they do (connection between feelings, thoughts, and behavior), and how their actions affect others (social impact and perspective-taking).

Self-awareness can manifest in various situations and circumstances. Recognition plays a role as a student may say, "I'm feeling frustrated with a math problem; I need to take a break." The student might say, "This is hard, but I will ask for help." Self-awareness is the student understanding their learning style, stress patterns, or motivators. Self-awareness is the building block for other social emotional learning skills because students can't regulate what they cannot recognize.

Resilience, with self-awareness as a foundational block, has many looks. It may look like a student trying again after receiving a low grade. It could look like a student recovering from conflict with a classmate. It could look like a student trying to navigate change at home or school with a trusted teacher, coach, even administrator. It could look like a student believing their efforts can create a better future.

Let's ask a question. How does self-awareness build resilience? When students can identify emotions, triggers, and strengths, they are more equipped to:

- Make application of coping strategies that work for them

- Hesitate before reacting impulsively
- Promote their own needs
- Contemplate on difficulties without self-disgust
- Repair their confidence after setbacks

Research abounds with information on how when students are enveloped in trauma-informed environments, self-awareness becomes a protective factor, giving them a sense of agency when life feels uncertain. Goleman (1995) explains that resilient individuals are able to advocate for themselves, engage in effective problem solving, and to seek support when they need it most.

Why These Skills Matter in Schools

Students with strong self-awareness and resilience are more likely to:

- Engage in learning even when lessons are difficult
- Resolve struggles without escalation
- Form positive relationships with peers and adults
- Endure through academic adversity
- Regulate emotions in healthy ways instead of through dysregulated behavior

The second pillar is **connection and support**: Connection is characteristic of good relationships with family, friends, and teachers. Support from an emotional and instructional standpoint aids students with development of skills to navigate adversity. Resilience can be seen when children are involved in community, cultural, and school engagement. Connection and support based upon authentic relationships with trusted people provide encouragement, perspective, and belonging during times of adversity. In fact, connection is one of Alison Block's 5 protective factors that promote resilience (Block, 2021).

FACING AND OVERCOMING ADVERSITY

Connection matters and is a strong predictor of resilience in children. Connection acts as a buffer against stress, trauma, and academic pressure. When students feel connected and supported, they experience:

- Increased emotional safety
- Better self – regulation
- Higher engagement and attendance
- Stronger identity and sense of belonging
- Reduced behavioral challenges

Support comes in many forms that build resilience. There's emotional support, academic and instructional support, and social support. Students provided emotional support receive it by way of warmth, empathy, and active listening. When students have predictable routines and direction provided by school faculty they can trust, great things happen.

Resilience is built when faculty provides clear expectations, scaffolding is used, and skill-building is learned in the classroom. Teachers play a role that cannot be denied, nor demised.

Resilience, lastly, is built on peer connections (peers learning and growing together), collaborative learning (students working together in pairs or groups), and restorative (strengthens relationships, build community, and create environments where students feel valued, heard, and connected) implemented on a consistent basis.

The third pillar is **<u>Purpose and meaning</u>** – Having a sense of "why" fuels perseverance. Purpose turns pain into motivation and struggle into growth. When students understand why their pursuit of education matters, they are more apt to persevere. When the work of fulfilling dreams, and goals challenge students purpose becomes their fuel to keep going even though they feel overwhelmed. Further, purpose strengthens students drive, and increases their willingness to try again after failure occurs.

Purpose gives direction when adversity arises. Resilience motivates a student to recover and reorient after a challenge, failure, defeat. They know what's necessary as they make sense of the setbacks, and are more likely to see failure as feedback rather than final. Purpose builds identify and promotes a sense of self-worth. Students with purpose internalize, then view themselves as competent, capable, and valuable. Students with purpose say things like, "I can handle this," "I'm pressing on towards something much bigger than what's happening right now."

As a kid growing up in inner-city of Cleveland, I found it necessary to have purpose for everything I did. It didn't matter if it was running track, playing football or passionately engaged in a friendly game of electric football with my cousins (Eric Anderson and Darryl Anderson). Not knowing that resilience was the reason behind my purposeful drive, I was one to not give up easily because my "why" was bigger than obstacles before me. Purpose fueled my persistence, especially when whatever I was doing became difficult.

Hope is another ingredient of resilience, in fact, hope anchors resilience. A student with purpose has a reason to believe in the possibility of a promising future even when present circumstances are prevailing. A great example of resilience anchored by hope is meeting a young teenager at Choffin Career & Technical Center in the fall of 2024. She'd been kicked out of her home by her parents. She was living from pillar to post. What caught my attention was that she was happy, socially engaged with peers, focused on attending Ohio State University, although sleeping on her boyfriend's couch. I was looking for anger, anxiety, bitterness and resentment but found resilience anchored by hope. Psychologist Chan Hellman believes hope is measurable and, therefore, predictive of success (Hellman, 2018). Purpose turns challenges into stepping stones, not a derailment. It helps students navigate beyond the moment, believe in their potential, and continue moving forward with strength and clarity.

The fourth pillar is **Adaptability and problem-solving** – This has a focus on how students adjust, stay flexible, and find solutions when life isn't going as planned. This pillar of resilience is then rooted and grounded in a sense of self, strengthened by connection, guided by purpose, and sustained by adaptability.

Students, with help, can realize that everything is not a failure, setback or threat. One doesn't have to be a rocket scientist to know that adaptability is a challenge for many students, especially grades k -12. When students learn and make practical application of being adaptable their ability to be resilient will improve exponentially.

Adaptability is critical for students for many reasons. Let's consider a student moving to another school district. The student will have to adapt to a new bus to ride, new peers to meet, and even a new curriculum to learn in the classroom. Surely this student will leave home feeling anxious about the new school. The student must navigate the thoughts, feelings, and anxiety adjustments, way of thinking, and how to move forward and ultimately adapt.

Adaptability will help students deal with the change that so often happens in their lives. Routines will shift, expectations change, and unexpected challenges occur. When they can adapt it strengthens their resilience. It teaches students that sometimes changes happen, that being flexible is critical, and that change can be handled.

Problem-solving goes hand in hand with adaptability. It gives students the ability to deal with barriers head on. Strategy replaces panic allowing students to build a robust resilience. Students become better equipped to break challenges into manageable steps. Students, when having problem-solving skills, are able to think through options in challenging times and deal with the consequences of their decisions. A student with problem-solving skills learns from their mistakes, allowing resilience to take center stage by not giving up.

In a nutshell we can be clear that adaptability assist students with facing change. On the other hand, problem-solving assist and helps students manage their challenges. When you put both together, they form a solid backbone of resilience.

Chapter 6 – Identifying and Understanding Risk and Protective Factors

Promoting resilience calls for an understanding of the protective and risk factors in a young person's life. Protective factors enhance the probability that a student will be resilient and mollify negative influences. Alternatively, risk factors can form hurdles and impede a student's ability to develop resilience.

Academic institutions play a central part in actuating student's resilience. Students spend countless hours, five days a week, in or around the classroom. As a result, schools can be contributory in providing protective factors and limiting risk factors for their students.

Further, Identifying and understanding risk and protective factors are central to building resilient students. These factors influence how students respond to adversity, manage stress, and develop the internal strength to thrive despite challenges in and out of the classroom.

Resilience is inhibited by risk factors and promoted by protective factors (Alvord & Grados, 2005; Benzies & Mychasiuk, 2009; Fergus & Zimmerman, 2005; Martinez-Torteya, Bogat, von Eye, & Levendosky, 2009; Masten et al., 1991; Rak & Patterson, 1996; Walsh, 2003). Protective factors alter responses to adverse events so that potential negative outcomes can be avoided. On the other hand, risk factors are circumstances that increase the probability of poor outcomes. Protective and risk factors are not stationary units; they change in relation to context leading to different outcomes (Walsh, 2003).

Risk factors are conditions or influences that increase the likelihood of negative outcomes. Risk Factors manifest in various ways to name a few there is trauma, poverty and socioeconomic challenges. There is violence, parental substance abuse, and lack of access to resources. There is negative family dynamics, family, and health issues. There is bullying, limited opportunities for positive experiences, and lack of social-emotional learning.

The aforementioned risk factors play a significant role regardless of where a student lives and/or how they may be parented. Students can have high GPA's even low GPA's and still be enveloped by risk factors. Students, whether m two parent families or broken homes, can still encounter risk factors that can create academic stress, poor coping skills, and academic struggles.

Many factors play a role in risk factors challenging our students in and out of the classroom. In the first-place risk factors can be a detriment. Risk factors can cause students to disengage academically, have poor attendance, which currently plagues our schools across the country. Students with high risk factors, not helped, are prone to drop out. Often times students dealing with risk factors don't have the support at home necessary to work through, and/or overcome academic challenges. Limited resources can impact students especially when they have limited resources such as books, after-school help, and use of technology.

In the second place, there are emotional and mental health effects that cause anxiety, depression, and bullying to name a few (Esch, P., Bocquet, V., Pull, C., et al. (2014). The downward spiral of mental disorders and educational attainment. Social Psychiatry and Psychiatric Epidemiology, 49, 129-139. Often times students have difficulty staying focused and their ability to process information is manifested. Many times, students can engage in "learned helplessness," as they often communicate a lack of belief in their abilities.

In the third place, many at risk students show behavior not conducive to classroom learning. There's aggression, defiance, and many times withdrawal from peers. At risk students have difficulty staying in school (suspensions) even disciplinary actions. Many times, teachers label these students saying, "they are incorrigible, unmotivated, and troubled." There's no doubt that when students can't communicate what they're feeling, behavior is the by product.

In the fourth place, many students are challenged socially. When students grow up in homes that are unstable (single parents, poor environments) they struggle to form good/healthy relationships. Many times, we will see students, whom have not been able to navigate risk factors, feel out of touch with peers, experience rejection, and exclusion. Being socially connected in school forms a protective umbrella, helping students be less vulnerable.

In the fifth place, when students are experiencing risk factors, their ability to hope and be resilient is weakened leading to poor self-actualization, difficulty working through problems, and an inability to forecast their futures. Hope is looking beyond the horizon to see the shore of possibilities. Dreams and goals are empowered by hope and resilience.

Finally, there is a cumulative effect on students when risk factors overwhelm them. I've seen many students in Youngstown City School District show symptoms of stress, emotional overload, even being overwhelmed by challenges they should be able to navigate.

Risk factors don't define a student but they can limit their opportunities unless balanced by protective factors like support, relationships, and resilience building environments.

Protective factors are conditions or influences that buffer against risk, promote resilience, and support positive outcomes. Schools and mental health establishments can help produce students who are healthy and resilient by being calculated, systematic, and complementary in their approach. When teaching/mental health practitioners build protective factors into students' everyday life, risky behaviors such as substance abuse, violence, and school dropout can substantially be diminished.

There is no question about the positive influence protective factors have on building a foundation of resilience in students. Not a day goes by while driving to my office at Choffin Career & Technical Center (Youngstown City School District) that I don't brood over ways to be a positive influence in the lives of the scholars (students are called scholars in our district) within my spacial order or proximity. So, lets peruse the landscape of protective factors that build resilience in children and students alike. I'm mindful that research has indicated many protective factors however, I will account for those that promote resilience in students.

Relationship is a protective factor that seems to make its way to the top of any protective factors list when related to resilience in students. Parents, family and teachers, coaches are the adults who daily play a role in the process of building and promoting resilience. Then there's community, cultural, and faith-based relationships that promote resilience. When students are able to internalize the aforementioned relationships, they find connectedness which promotes resilience.

FACING AND OVERCOMING ADVERSITY

Kirsten Weir says, "Researchers agree that of all the factors that boost resilience, good parenting is often the most significant" (Weir, 2017, p. 40). Phillip Fisher, Ph.D. a professor of psychology at the University of Oregon, says, "The biggest difference, over and above one's genetic blueprint, is the relationship a child has with a primary caregiver." Time and time again I've seen students who are resilient and exhibit resilient tendencies and at the core of their resilience is a parent, or adult figure. I'm a living witness of the quotes by Weir and Fisher that resilience is boosted by good parenting. My mother (Verta Freeman) continuously said to me, "Always give your best at whatever you do," my grandmother (Bertha Anderson) would say, "Remember the little engine that said I think I can," and my high school track coach and consummate educator (James Patterson) who would say, "Natural ability will take you but so far, hard work will take you further." All the previous mentioned individuals played vital roles in promoting my resilience.

Being an example promotes resilience by modeling attitudes, behaviors, and coping strategies you, as a teacher, or any adult for that matter, want students to develop. By promoting resilience students are given a living blueprint for how to navigate adversity. Children learn far more from what teachers demonstrate than from what they declare, and consistent, authentic modeling becomes a powerful source of emotional and behavioral guidance.

When teachers and caregivers model calm problem-solving, flexible thinking, and healthy emotional expression, students begin to internalize those same skills. A student observing a teacher handle stress with composure, acknowledge mistakes without shame, and persevere through challenges shows them that setbacks are not signs of failure but opportunities to grow. This builds confidence and reduces fear of trying, failing, and trying again.

Likewise, when adults model empathy, inclusivity, and respectful communication, students learn how to build strong relationships, which is one of the strongest predictors of resilience. Modeling also creates psychological safety: when students watch teachers/adults own their emotions, repair harm, or ask for help, they realize that vulnerability is not weakness but strength.

Ultimately, being an example gives students a real-life roadmap for resilience. It shows them what resilience looks like in action and empowers them to mirror those behaviors in their own lives, helping them develop the internal tools needed to thrive despite challenges.

Shaping the environment is a protective factor that builds resilience. Although many factors predisposing resilience are intrinsic, developing resilience necessitates a multilayered and unified approach. The school plays a significant role in students learning ecosystem. Schools must provide an environment conducive to a positive environment. Students should be afforded consistent, predictable, and clear expectations and boundaries that allow them to thrive. When the culture and climate of a school is positive, and optimistic it should and will produce resilient students.

I'm thrilled every time I enter Rayen Early College Middle School in Youngstown City School District. This is because the culture and climate of the school exudes consistency, is predictable, and the positive atmosphere lends itself to a learning ecosystem. The principal (Dr. Maureen Donofrio and faculty) begins from day one of the school year creating and maintaining an environment that every student can learn to abide within. The students enjoy the learning process, build positive relationships, and continuously produce grades indicative of an environment that has been shaped for success.

Communication is a vital protective factor that strengthens resilience by nurturing connection, clarity, and coping in students.

FACING AND OVERCOMING ADVERSITY

When young people are encouraged to express their thoughts and emotions openly, they develop a sense of belonging and trust that anchors them during challenging moments.

Clear and compassionate communication from teachers, or any adult, reduces confusion and stress, creating an environment where students feel safe to ask questions, make mistakes, and seek support. As students learn to articulate their needs, navigate conflict, and engage in collaborative problem-solving they build the social and emotional skills that empower them to adapt in times of adversity. Over time, the supportive language they hear becomes the positive inner voice that fuels their confidence, persistence, and hope. In this way, communication does far more than exchange information, it cultivates the conditions in which resilience can truly grow.

Establishing a culture of inclusivity promotes resilience in K–12 students by constructing a climate where every student can experience a sense of being valued, accepted, and supported. This is a key point in helping students deal with adversity. When students experience a sense of belonging, they are more likely to engage, take academic risks, and trust the adults around them.

Inclusivity reduces feelings of isolation, which is one of the greatest barriers to resilience, and instead fosters psychological safety—a foundation that allows students to express emotions, seek help, and try again after setbacks. In inclusive classrooms, diverse perspectives and backgrounds are honored, teaching students empathy, perspective-taking, and collaborative problem-solving skills. These experiences help them navigate social challenges with confidence.

Furthermore, inclusivity ensures that students see themselves reflected in the curriculum, the environment, and the school culture, reinforcing positive identity development and strengthening their internal sense of worth. Ultimately, a culture of inclusivity builds a supportive network around students, equipping them with the emotional, social, and relational resources needed to thrive despite the challenges they face.

Self-control promotes resilience in students because it equips them with the ability to manage their emotions, behaviors, and impulses when faced with challenges. When students develop self-control, they learn to pause before reacting, giving themselves space to choose responses that support problem-solving rather than escalate stress. This ability to regulate emotions helps them stay grounded during difficult moments, reducing the likelihood of feeling overwhelmed or defeated.

Self-control also strengthens resilience by empowering students to persist toward long-term goals even when short-term frustrations arise. Students who can refocus their attention, delay gratification, and resist distractions are better able to stay engaged academically and socially, which builds confidence and a sense of capability.

Additionally, practicing self-control helps students navigate conflicts more peacefully, maintain positive relationships, and recover more quickly from setbacks—core components of resilience. Ultimately, self-control gives students the internal tools to weather adversity with clarity and composure. It allows them to manage stress, make wise choices, and keep moving forward, which forms a strong foundation for resilient thinking and behavior.

Knowing and building rapport with your students does not grow in isolation; it grows in relationship. One of the most powerful ways educators can strengthen resilience in K–12 students is by intentionally getting to know who their students are, not just academically, but socially, emotionally, and culturally. When teachers understand the whole child, they create learning spaces

FACING AND OVERCOMING ADVERSITY

where students feel seen, valued, and supported. That sense of connection becomes a protective factor that equips students to navigate adversity with confidence.

When students feel known, they experience psychological safety, and the emotional assurance that school is a place where they can take risks, make mistakes, and recover without fear of judgment. This safety opens the door for persistence. A child who trusts their teacher is more willing to try again after failure, more open to feedback, and more capable of regulating emotions in moments of challenge.

Resilience comes by knowing and building rapport with students also builds a deep sense of belonging, which research identifies as one of the strongest predictors of resilience. Belonging communicates, "You matter here." For students carrying trauma, facing instability at home, or struggling socially, a building and classroom environment where they are understood becomes a stabilizing force. Connection is the antidote to isolation, and students who feel connected are more likely to rebound during stressful seasons. I love what Dr. Brene Brown says about connectedness, "I define connection as the energy that exists between people when they feel seen, heard, and valued, when they can give and receive without judgment; and when they derive sustenance and strength from the relationship."

Understanding students' backgrounds, communication styles, and triggers equips educators to respond rather than react. When a teacher knows the story behind a behavior, they shift from punishment to support. Instead of escalating conflict, they guide students through emotional regulation, reflection, and repair skills that resides at the heart of resilience. Knowing and building rapport helps students learn that challenges do not define them; instead, each challenge becomes an opportunity to build stronger coping strategies.

Additionally, knowing students enables teachers to tailor instruction to their strengths and interests, making learning more engaging and meaningful. Personalized motivation fuels persistence. When students see themselves reflected in the curriculum, or when assignments connect to their passions, they are more likely to stay committed through academic struggles.

When an educator honors students' culture, identity, and lived experiences, they strengthen each child's internal sense of worth. A strong identity functions like armor during adversity. Students who know they are valued and who see that their teacher respects who they are should approach challenges with greater confidence, optimism, and hope.

Finally, knowing your students is not a soft skill; it is a resilience strategy. It transforms the classroom from a place of compliance into a community of belonging. It moves teachers from managing behavior to nurturing growth. It ensures that every student, regardless of background, has at least one caring adult investing in their success. When students feel known, they feel safe. When they feel safe, they can learn, take risks, and rise.

Chapter 7 – Adversity as a Teacher: Understanding How Adversity Shapes Resilience

Adversity is often viewed as something to avoid, minimize, or escape. In the lives of students, adversity can show up as academic setbacks, social challenges, family instability, trauma, poverty, or moments of disappointment that press against a child's sense of safety and confidence. While adversity can create barriers to learning, it also carries another truth: adversity can teach, develop, and strengthen the internal skills that form the foundation of resilience. When educators understand adversity, not as a punishment but as a process, they can help students transform difficult experiences into opportunities for growth.

Resilience is not built in comfortable, predictable seasons. It is shaped in moments when students face something they are not sure they can handle. When students receive support, guidance, and encouragement along the way they can overcome adversity and develop resilience that will help them throughout the lifespan. When a child navigates adversity with a caring adult by their side, their brain develops new pathways for problem-solving, emotional regulation, and hope. They begin to learn, "I can do hard things. I can survive difficult moments. I can rise again."

Adversity Builds Inner Strength

Adversity challenges students to stretch beyond their comfort zones. When students encounter frustration in academics, conflicts with peers, or changes in their environment, they learn to manage stress in real time. These experiences strengthen persistence, patience, and adaptability. Each moment of struggle becomes a rehearsal for future challenges. Instead of breaking students, adversity, when supported helps build the emotional muscles that make them stronger.

Adversity Teaches Problem-Solving

When students face obstacles, their brains must shift from reaction to reflection. They begin asking: What are my options? Who can help me? How can I approach this differently?

These questions strengthen executive functioning skills essential for lifelong resilience. Students learn to pause, think, evaluate choices, and make decisions. These skills will serve them not only in school but in relationships, careers, and adulthood.

Adversity Develops Emotional Regulation

Hard moments trigger strong emotions, from frustration to fear. But with the support of a trusted adult, students learn how to identify, express, and manage those emotions in healthy ways. They discover that emotions are signals, not threats. This emotional regulation becomes one of the most powerful resilience tools a student can acquire. A child who can calm themselves, re-center, and continue forward has a lifelong advantage.

Adversity Reveals Identity and Purpose

Adversity often becomes the mirror that helps students see who they are and what they are capable of. When they overcome a difficult moment—no matter how small—they discover internal qualities such as courage, perseverance, and determination. Adversity shows students that their story is not defined by challenges but by how they rise from them. This deepens identity, cultivates confidence, and builds a sense of purpose.

Adversity Builds Empathy and Compassion

Students who have faced adversity often develop a heightened awareness of others' struggles. They become more empathetic, more patient, and more capable of offering support to peers. Adversity softens the heart even as it strengthens the mind. It helps students understand that everyone is carrying something and that kindness can make someone else's burden feel lighter.

Teaches Students the Power of Relationships

Children learn resilience not in isolation but in connection. Adversity teaches them that it is okay to ask for help, lean on others, and trust supportive adults. The presence of even one caring adult during adversity can change a student's entire life trajectory. When educators walk alongside students during hard moments, they reinforce the truth that resilience is not built alone—it's built-in community.

Adversity Helps Students Develop Hope

The greatest lesson adversity teaches is hope. When a student encounters a challenge, works through it, and comes out stronger, they learn that setbacks are temporary. They learn to look beyond the moment they are in. Hope becomes the anchor that keeps them grounded during future storms. When students believe that tomorrow holds possibility, resilience becomes their natural response to difficulty.

The Role of Educators in the Adversity-Resilience Cycle

Educators hold a vital role in how students interpret and respond to adversity. Teachers can't remove every challenge, but they can influence whether adversity becomes a barrier or a bridge. When teachers respond with patience, empathy, structure, and encouragement, they help students transform overwhelming moments into empowering ones. Educators become interpreters—helping students understand that adversity is not the end of the story but the beginning of growth. Students learn resilience when an adult says,

"I see your struggle. I believe in you. I'm here to help you through this."

Conclusion: Adversity Is the Classroom of the Heart

In every school, adversity walks through the doors with the students. But adversity does not have to be the villain in the story. It can become the teacher—the one that develops courage, shapes character, and strengthens resilience. With supportive adults, safe environments, and intentional teaching, adversity becomes a catalyst that empowers students to rise stronger, think deeper, and hope brighter. When educators understand how adversity shapes resilience, they become builders of strength, mentors of perseverance, and guides who help students discover the resilience they did not know they had.

CHAPTER 8 – EDUCATOR RESILIENCE: THE HEARTBEAT OF A THRIVING SCHOOL

Teaching has always been more than a profession. It is emotional labor, community work, relational leadership, and mission-driven service woven together. Educators carry the weight of students' academic needs, social–emotional challenges, personal stories, trauma histories, and daily uncertainties. Despite these demands, thousands of teachers continue to show up with courage, compassion, and creativity. What sustains them? Resilience.

Defining educator resilience, in its broader context is, "The capacity to bounce back, to recover strength or spirit quickly and efficiently in the face of adversity, and it is closely linked with vocational commitment, self-efficacy, and the motivation to teach" (Sammons et al., 2007, p. 694). Psychology Today says, "Resilience isn't just about coping. It's about sustaining passion, maintaining purpose, and navigating adversity without losing oneself. And as we face escalating complexities in schools—whether it's post-pandemic mental health surges, digital transformation, or staffing crises—resilience may be our most vital asset" Psychology Today, 2025).

Educator resilience is not about perfection, toughness, or never feeling stressed. It is the ongoing process of adapting, recovering, and growing through the challenges inherent in education. It is the internal capacity and external support that allow educators to continue doing meaningful work without losing themselves in the process. Resilience keeps teachers grounded when circumstances change, hopeful when outcomes seem uncertain, and steady when students need stability most.

The Nature of Resilience in Educators

Resilience can manifest in K-12 educators through behaviors that prioritize emotional steadiness, connection, and adaptability. It is visible in how they show up, how they respond, how they recover, and how they continue to care. When educators demonstrate resilience, they not only sustain themselves, they shape the culture of the school, and strengthen their student's capacity to overcome adversity. Resilience is not a trait someone either has or does not have. It is a dynamic skill set shaped by experiences, relationships, beliefs, and environments. For educators, resilience emerges at the intersection of purpose, competence, connection, and well-being.

1. Purpose: <u>The Anchor</u>

Purpose provides educators with a clear "why" that steadies them in the midst of daily challenges. Purpose gives educators the stamina to deal with behavioral issues, shifting expectations, emotional demands, and the weight of supporting students who carry their own adversity. When educators understand the deeper meaning behind their work, setbacks feel less like roadblocks and more like reminders of the importance of their role.

Purpose sustains passion, fuels perseverance, and helps educators recover more quickly from stress because they know their efforts contribute to something larger than the moment. It grounds them, guides their decisions, and becomes the internal compass that keeps them steady when the work becomes overwhelming. In this way, purpose is not just motivation, it is the foundation upon which educator resilience is built.

2. Competence: The Confidence to Act

Competence helps a teacher be resilient because it strengthens confidence, reduces stress, and equips them to navigate challenges with clarity. When educators develop strong skills in instruction, classroom management, relationship-building, and problem-solving, they feel more capable of handling the unpredictable nature of K–12 environments. Competence creates a sense of mastery. Educators trust their own professional judgment and are less shaken by setbacks or difficult situations when they possess the tools necessary to deal with the myriad of situations and circumstances that await them. Instead of feeling overwhelmed, they can draw from proven strategies and past successes to adapt, adjust, and move forward. This competence also boosts emotional resilience; when teachers know they can handle it, they are more likely to remain calm, reflective, and solution-focused. Ultimately, competence provides the tools and self-assurance teachers need to withstand challenges and continue showing up effectively for their students.

3. Connection: The Protective Factor

Connection is a powerful engine of resilience for educators because it strengthens the emotional and professional bonds that sustain them through difficult seasons. When educators feel connected to colleagues, leaders, students, and the broader school community they are less likely to experience the isolation that often leads to burnout. These relationships create a network of shared wisdom where teachers can exchange strategies, process challenges, and gain perspective that helps them rebound more quickly from stress.

Connection also provides emotional grounding; having trusted people to talk with regulates stress, restores hope, and reminds teachers of their purpose. Ultimately, connected teachers feel supported, valued, and anchored, making them more capable of navigating adversity while maintaining the heart and stamina required to teach well.

4. *Well-Being: <u>The Foundation</u>*

Well-being is a foundational aspect of educator resilience because it sustains the physical, emotional, and mental resources teachers need to navigate the demands of the classroom. When educators prioritize their well-being, through adequate rest, healthy boundaries, emotional regulation, supportive relationships, and purposeful reflection they build the inner capacity required to respond to challenges rather than become overwhelmed by them.

An educator's well-being strengthens resilience by protecting against burnout, enhancing clarity in decision-making, and increasing the ability to adapt in moments of stress. It also fuels the patience, empathy, and composure needed to support students who may be experiencing their own adversity. Ultimately, teacher well-being is not a luxury; it is a critical component of resilient practice, allowing educators to show up with consistency, creativity, and compassion even in difficult circumstances.

Pressures That Test Educator Resilience

Every school year brings unique stressors that challenge even the most measured educators. These pressures may include:

- Rising academic and behavioral needs in a post-pandemic landscape
- Increased expectations without proportional support
- Compassion fatigue from carrying students' trauma
- Shifting policies and curriculum mandates
- Lack of resources or staffing shortages
- Navigating conflict within school communities

These realities do not indicate weakness but reveal the human cost of caregiving professions like teaching. Resilience requires acknowledging the weight of the work, not denying it.

How Resilient Educators Respond to Adversity

Resilience shows up in how educators navigate challenges. Resilient educators demonstrate:

Emotional Regulation

They stay grounded when students are dysregulated, understanding that calm is contagious.

Adaptability

They shift approaches rather than giving up, finding creative solutions to daily problems.

Reflective Practice

They ask, "What can I learn from this?" instead of "Why is this happening to me?"

Help-Seeking

They reach out to colleagues, counselors, and leadership rather than attempting to carry everything alone.

Hopeful Outlook

They maintain a belief that students can grow, situations can improve, and challenges are temporary. These behaviors are not innate as they can be taught, modeled, and strengthened over time.

School Culture as a Catalyst for Educator Resilience

Individual resilience is powerful, but it cannot flourish in an unhealthy system. Schools that promote resilience intentionally cultivate:

Psychological Safety

Educators feel safe to ask for help, try new ideas, and admit mistakes.

Restorative Relationships

Staff resolve conflict through empathy, accountability, and connection—not blame.

Supportive Leadership

Administrators communicate clearly, provide feedback, and recognize effort and growth.

Professional Autonomy

Educators have input in decision-making and flexibility in instructional strategies.

Collaboration

No one teaches alone. Teams share resources, problem-solve, and encourage one another.

When schools invest in these practices, resilience becomes a collective strength rather than an individual burden.

Why Educator Resilience Matters for Students

Student's do not learn well from adults who are overwhelmed, exhausted, or emotionally depleted. A resilient educator:

- Models emotional regulation and coping skills
- Creates a predictable, calm classroom climate
- Builds trusting relationships that become protective factors
- Maintains high expectations paired with strong support

- Demonstrates perseverance, hope, and problem-solving (skills students mirror)

When educators thrive, students thrive.

Building Educator Resilience: Practical Strategies

1. Prioritize Self-Compassion

Acknowledge limitations, celebrate small wins, and practice grace with yourself.

2. Develop a Regulation Plan

Identify strategies (breathing, mindfulness, stepping away) to restore calm during stress.

3. Engage in Reflective Practice

Journaling, coaching conversations, or peer debriefs to deepen insight and growth.

4. Strengthen Professional Community

Connection reduces burnout and expands collective resilience.

5. Advocate for Healthy Systems

Seek supports, request training, and participate in shaping school culture.

6. Maintain Purpose

Regularly revisit what brought you to education and what keeps you there.

A Closing Word: Resilience Is a journey

Educator resilience is not a finish line. It is a lifelong practice shaped by seasons, experiences, and relationships. There will be moments of strength and moments of struggle. But resilience grows when educators remain connected to purpose, supported by community, and committed to caring for themselves with the same compassion they extend to students.

A resilient educator does more than withstand adversity. They transform it, and in doing so, they become a powerful force of stability, hope, and possibility in the lives of the children they serve.

Chapter 9 - Resilience as a Necessity in Today's Educational Climate

Teaching in an Era of Uncertainty

Today's educators stand at the intersection of unprecedented change, persistent social stressors, and escalating expectations. Schools are not simply academic institutions; they are emotional hubs, trauma-response centers, stability anchors, and spaces where hope must be cultivated daily. In such a complex ecosystem, teacher resilience is not a luxury or admirable trait—it is a professional necessity. Resilient teachers sustain their sense of purpose, remain grounded during instability, and serve as the emotional thermostat for their classrooms and school communities.

The Educational Landscape and the Pressure on Educators

Modern teaching exists within a climate defined by:

- Increased student mental health needs and trauma exposure
- Academic pressure tied to accountability, performance metrics, and policy shifts
- Societal disruptions (violence, inequity, community stressors, pandemics, technological shifts)
- Workforce instability (teacher shortages, burnout, attrition)
- Intensified emotional demands (supporting families, navigating trauma, relational repair work)

This climate can erode teacher well-being, creating exhaustion, cynicism, and detachment—conditions that directly undermine educational quality. Without resilience, educators can become overwhelmed, reactive instead of reflective, and disconnected from their "why."

Why Teacher Resilience Matters for Students

Resilience is not only about teacher survival—it directly impacts student outcomes. When teachers are well, regulated, hopeful, and psychologically present:

- Students feel psychologically safe
- Learning environments become emotionally predictable
- Instructional quality improves
- Restorative responses replace punitive reactions
- Relationships deepen
- Students learn resilience through modeling

Students learn resilience not only from curricula, but from people. A resilient teacher models' adaptability, emotional regulation, coping, problem solving, empathy, and perseverance. In many cases, the teacher becomes the clearest illustration of how to navigate adversity with dignity and strength.

Resilient Teachers Protect Their Calling and Purpose

Teaching is purpose-driven work. It requires passion, emotional investment, intellectual commitment, and relational energy. Yet purpose without resilience leads to burnout. Resilience allows educators to:

- Remain anchored in meaning despite difficulty
- Maintain hope while working with struggling students
- Rebound when lessons fail or progress feels slow
- Continue believing in students when others do not
- Stay connected to joy, humor, and humanity in the work

In essence, resilience protects the educator's heart while preserving the effectiveness of their craft.

Resilience Strengthens Instruction, Creativity, and Problem Solving

Teaching demands flexibility. Students learn differently, needs shift rapidly, and what worked one year may not work the next.

Resilient educators demonstrate:

- Cognitive flexibility – adapting instruction rather than becoming rigid
- Innovation – trying new strategies rather than giving up
- Reflective practice – learning from failure rather than internalizing defeat
- Solution orientation – focusing on what can be done

Classrooms led by resilient educators are dynamic, responsive, and intellectually alive.

Resilience Supports Trauma-Informed and Restorative Practice

Today's schools must simultaneously educate and heal. Teachers working with students facing adversity must navigate emotional outbursts, dysregulation, withdrawal, and behavioral disruptions.

Without emotional resilience:

- Teachers become reactive
- Punitive discipline increases
- Relationships are fracture
- Students internalize rejection rather than restoration

Resilient teachers, however, can remain regulated, compassionate, and consistent. They practice curiosity rather than judgment. They maintain connection even when behavior disappoints. They understand that behavior communicates need and resilience sustains the patience required to meet that need.

Teacher Well-Being is a Professional Responsibility

Teacher resilience is not self-indulgence; it is professional commitment. Schools flourish when educators flourish. Resilient teachers exhibit:

- Emotional regulation
- Healthy boundaries
- Self-awareness
- Willingness to seek support
- Commitment to continuous learning
- Capacity to recover rather than collapse

Mentally, psychologically, and emotionally "attuned" educators create well classrooms. Burned-out educators inadvertently transmit stress to students. Resilience ensures that teachers do not simply "show up," but show up with clarity, empathy, strength, and purpose.

School Culture Improves When Teachers Are Resilient

School climate is not built by policies alone—it is built by people. Resilient teachers contribute to:

- Collaborative, trusting staff environments
- Positive staff morale
- Shared problem solving rather than blaming
- Stability during change or crisis
- A culture of hope

They become emotional anchors for colleagues, team stabilizers, and leaders who foster safety and unity.

Resilience and Retention: Keeping Strong Educators in the Profession

Teacher attrition has become a national crisis. Many educators leave not because they lack skill, but because they are exhausted.

Resilience increases:

- Career longevity
- Professional satisfaction
- Commitment to the mission
- Capacity to remain in challenging schools

When resilient teachers remain, students benefit from experience, continuity, mentorship, and institutional memory.

How Teachers Build and Sustain Resilience

Resilience is not a personality trait—it is a practiced capacity. It can be strengthened through intentional habits:

1. Connection – supportive colleagues, mentors, community
2. Purpose Alignment – remembering why the work matters
3. Reflection – learning from difficulty instead of internalizing defeat
4. Self-regulation – practices that calm the nervous system
5. Healthy Boundaries – understanding that "rest is resistance" and protection
6. Professional Learning – skill building that increases confidence
7. Hope Practices – gratitude, reframing, celebrating growth

Resilient teachers do not simply endure hardship—they grow through it, innovate because of it, and lead in spite of it.

Resilient Teachers Build Resilient Students

Every resilient student has, somewhere in their journey, encountered a resilient adult who believed, supported, guided, and stayed in their life. In today's educational climate, teacher resilience sustains hope, strengthens instruction, stabilizes school culture, and protects the emotional health of students. When teachers thrive, students thrive. When educators remain grounded, compassionate, and resilient, they do far more than teach content—they shape lives, restore dignity, inspire perseverance, and build the next generation of resilient human beings.

Chapter 10 – Teaching Student's to Name Their Feelings and Needs

Teaching students to name their feelings and needs is foundational to emotional intelligence and resilience. When children can identify what they feel and what they need, they are better able to regulate their behavior, communicate effectively, and seek support in healthy ways. This skill doesn't happen automatically as it must be modeled, practiced, and reinforced in intentional ways.

An illustration of this skill was seen with a student/athlete I coached in Middle School. She was participating in the track & field program. This particular student came to practice on a beautiful Spring Day. She laughed and clowned with the other athletes until it was time to warm up with the team. She then vacated to the bleachers to sit down. When asked why she shrugged her shoulders saying, "I don't know coach." I pushed further hoping for a different response, and I received that response with, "Coach, I'm not sure how to say what I'm feeling and need." Also, she said, "Please don't be upset with me."

After ensuring her I would not be angry with her, that it was safe to communicate whatever she was going through, she began to cry informing me that she had not slept the night before because of her mom and dad being engaged in domestic violence. The student shared that she was feeling overwhelmed and sad, that what she needed was a safe space, and something to eat. The track team and my oversight were her safe space. Further, she knew food was available therefore, what she was feeling and needed would be provided for her.

As I move forward talking about the need for teachers to teach this skill, I'm mindful this skill is not innate; it must be nurtured intentionally through modeling, language development, and consistent practice.

Students are far more likely to express their emotions when they feel connected to the adults around them. Trust is the foundation of emotional safety, and emotional safety is the foundation of authentic communication. When students know that a teacher cares, listens without judgment, and responds with consistency and respect, they begin to feel safe enough to name what is happening inside of them.

Strong relationships create an environment where students don't fear embarrassment, punishment, or dismissal. Instead, they experience the classroom as a place where their voices matter. This sense of security encourages them to pause, reflect, and communicate openly rather than act out their emotions through behavior. For many students, especially those with trauma histories, trust must be built slowly through predictable routines, reliable responses, and genuine interest in their well-being. Over time, relationship becomes the bridge that allows students to share their feelings and articulate their needs with confidence.

Ultimately, relationship and trust are not just helpful they are essential. They clear the path for emotional honesty, reduce the emotional load students carry, and create the conditions where learning and resilience can flourish.

Building an Emotional Vocabulary

Students can only name what they have language for. Too often, children operate with a limited set of emotional words, leaving them unable to express what is happening internally. Expanding their emotional vocabulary through feeling charts, classroom visuals, and direct instruction provides them with the tools they need to articulate their inner experiences. Introducing words such as discouraged, anxious, overwhelmed, hopeful, and curious gives students more accurate ways to express themselves and reduces the likelihood of misbehavior driven by emotional confusion.

The Power of Modeling

Adults play a crucial role in demonstrating what healthy emotional expression looks like. When teachers name their own emotions and needs in real time such as, "I'm feeling a bit rushed, and I need us to transition quietly" or "I'm excited about your progress and I need your attention" then students witness emotional regulation in action. This modeling normalizes emotional honesty and teaches students that naming feelings is a sign of strength, not weakness.

Routines That Build Emotional Awareness

Emotional check-ins provide structured opportunities for students to practice self-awareness daily. Tools such as mood meters, color zones, or simple one-word check-ins help students pause, reflect, and identify their current state. When teachers follow up with questions like "What do you need to be successful today?" students begin connecting emotions to actionable needs. Over time, these routines cultivate emotional intelligence and reduce reactive behaviors.

Connecting Feelings to Needs

A critical step in emotional development is helping students understand that every feeling carries a corresponding need. Anger may indicate a need for space or fairness. Anxiety might signal a need for reassurance or clarity. Frustration may point to a need for support or more time. Teaching this connection transforms emotions from overwhelming challenges into solvable problems. Students learn to ask for what they need rather than act out what they feel.

Using Stories and Scenarios as Safe Practice

Books, role-plays, and classroom scenarios offer safe, indirect opportunities for students to analyze emotions. When students identify what a character is feeling or what a peer might need, they strengthen their ability to recognize emotions in themselves. This practice deepens empathy and builds the foundation for restorative and compassionate classroom communities.

Validation as a Pathway to Trust

Students thrive when they know their feelings will be taken seriously. Validating students such as, "It makes sense you feel that way"—creates psychological safety and reduces the shame that often drives behavioral issues. Validation does not excuse inappropriate actions; instead, it opens the door for healthier choices by acknowledging the emotional reality beneath the behavior.

Restorative Conversations That Build Skill

When conflicts occur, restorative questions help students reflect, name emotions, and articulate needs. Questions such as "What were you feeling when that happened?" and "What do you need now to make things right?" turn difficult moments into emotional learning opportunities. These conversations teach students to communicate with honesty, empathy, and responsibility.

Structured Language for Clear Expression

Providing students with sentence starters gives them the scaffolding they need to express themselves. Phrases such as "I feel ___ because ___" and "Right now I need ___ so I can ___" empower students to communicate confidently and respectfully. With consistent use, these structures become internal tools students rely on throughout their academic and personal lives.

Creating a Culture Where It Is Safe to Speak

Students will only name their feelings when the classroom environment feels emotionally safe. A culture of respect, predictable routines, and adult responsiveness will encourage students to speak openly. When students know they won't be criticized, dismissed, or punished for expressing emotions, they develop the courage to share what they truly feel and need.

Why This Matters

Teaching students to name their feelings and needs builds the foundation for resilience. It promotes self-awareness, self-regulation, stronger relationships, and reduced conflict. For students navigating trauma, stress, or adversity, this skill is not simply helpful—it is life-changing. When students learn to understand their inner world, they gain the power to shape their outer world with confidence and purpose.

Chapter 11 – Creating A Resilient Classroom Environment

Resilience is the capacity to adapt, recover, and thrive in the face of challenges. In the context of education, fostering resilience in students is not just about helping them succeed academically—it's about equipping them with the social, emotional, and cognitive skills to navigate life's inevitable difficulties. A resilient classroom environment is one where students feel safe, valued, and empowered to take risks, make mistakes, and grow from them.

Creating such an environment requires intentionality from educators. It involves cultivating strong relationships, establishing consistent routines, promoting autonomy, and embedding social-emotional learning into daily practices. In classrooms designed for resilience, students learn to persevere through setbacks, manage stress, and develop a sense of agency over their learning. The result is not only academically capable students but individuals who can face challenges with confidence, adaptability, and hope. By understanding the key conditions that foster resilience, teachers can transform their classrooms into spaces where every student has the opportunity to flourish, both as a learner and as a resilient human being.

Fostering classrooms that produce resilient students has become more important, especially since the pandemic occurred. Researchers have found that, "A useful description of the classroom conditions allowing children to succeed despite the odds can be derived from the past seven decades of developmental research on risk and resilience" (Luthar & Eisenberg, 2017; Masten, 2014, 2018; Werner, 2013).

Classroom conditions that foster resilience focus on creating a supportive, predictable, and empowering environment where students can develop coping skills, confidence, and adaptability.

Here's a detailed breakdown:

1. *Safe and Predictable Environment*

- <u>Physical safety</u>: Clear rules, consistent routines, and a structured environment help students feel secure.

- <u>Emotional safety</u>: Students need to know they can express themselves without judgment. Teachers modeling calm, respectful behavior reinforce this.

- <u>Predictable routines</u>: Consistency reduces anxiety and allows students to focus on learning rather than survival.

Resilience grows best in a safe, predictable environment. When individuals know what to expect and feel emotionally and physically secure, their stress decreases and their capacity to cope increases. Consistent routines, clear expectations, and supportive relationships create stability, allowing people, especially children and students, to take healthy risks, regulate emotions, and recover more effectively from challenges. Safety and predictability do not eliminate adversity; they provide the foundation that helps individuals face it with confidence and strength.

2. *Strong Relationships and Connection*

- <u>Teacher-student trust</u>: Teachers who show genuine care, listen actively, and understand students' needs help build resilience.

- <u>Peer support</u>: Encouraging collaboration, empathy, and positive social interactions strengthens students' coping skills.

- Mentorship and modeling: Teachers and older peers who demonstrate problem-solving, perseverance, and self-regulation provide concrete examples of resilience.

Resilience is strengthened through healthy, supportive relationships. Trusted connections with caring adults, peers, and mentors provide emotional safety, encouragement, and guidance during times of stress or adversity. Relationships help individuals feel seen, valued, and understood along with key factors that foster hope and persistence. When challenges arise, strong relationships serve as a buffer against stress, reminding individuals that they are not alone and that support is available. In this way, connection is not just helpful to resilience—it is essential.

3. Opportunities for Autonomy and Agency

- Choice in learning: Allowing students to make decisions about tasks or projects builds confidence and a sense of control.
- Ownership of mistakes: Encouraging reflection and learning from errors fosters a growth mindset.
- Student voice: Including students in classroom decisions promotes responsibility and self-efficacy.

Resilience empowers individuals to exercise autonomy and agency by building confidence in their ability to face challenges and recover from setbacks. When people develop resilience, they learn that their choices matter and that they can influence outcomes through effort, problem-solving, and perseverance. This sense of competence encourages independent decision-making, responsible risk-taking, and self-advocacy. As resilience grows, individuals move from reacting to circumstances to actively shaping their path, strengthening both personal ownership and motivation.

4. Emphasis on Social-Emotional Learning

- <u>Emotion recognition and regulation</u>: Teaching students to identify and manage emotions supports coping under stress.

- <u>Problem-solving skills</u>: Explicitly teaching strategies to handle challenges increases adaptability.

- <u>Mindfulness and stress-reduction techniques</u>: Small practices can help students self-regulate in challenging situations.

Resilience and social-emotional learning are deeply interconnected. Social emotional learning builds the skills such as self-awareness, emotional regulation, empathy, and relationship-building those individuals need to respond effectively to stress and adversity. Resilience is the outcome of using those skills when challenges arise. As individuals practice naming emotions, managing reactions, solving problems, and seeking support, they become better equipped to adapt, persevere, and recover. Together, resilience and Social emotional learning creates a strong foundation for well-being, healthy relationships, and long-term success.

5. High Expectations with Support

- <u>Challenging yet achievable goals</u>: Students grow resilient when they face challenges with adequate support.

- <u>Feedback focused on effort</u>: Praising perseverance and strategies rather than innate ability builds persistence.

- <u>Scaffolded learning</u>: Step-by-step support helps students navigate difficulties without feeling overwhelmed.

Resilience is the bridge between high expectations and meaningful support. When individuals are held to high standards while receiving appropriate guidance, encouragement, and resources, they learn that challenges are not barriers but opportunities for growth. Support helps prevent discouragement, while high expectations communicate belief in one's ability. Resilience develops as individuals persevere through difficulty, learn from mistakes, and experience success with support. This balance fosters confidence, persistence, and a strong sense of capability with key elements of long-term growth and achievement.

6. Inclusive and Culturally Responsive Practices

- <u>Validation of identities</u>: Recognizing and respecting diverse backgrounds increases belonging and self-worth.

- <u>Equitable opportunities</u>: Ensuring all students can access learning and participate fully fosters resilience.

- <u>Responsive teaching</u>: Adjusting instruction to meet students' individual needs prevents repeated failure experiences.

Resilience strengthens inclusive and culturally responsive practices by honoring students' identities, experiences, and strengths as assets rather than deficits. When educators build resilience, they create environments where diverse voices are valued, cultural backgrounds are respected, and belonging is intentional. Culturally responsive practices reduce barriers to learning by fostering trust, psychological safety, and meaningful connection. This support helps students navigate adversity, develop confidence, and engage more fully. In turn, resilient learning communities empower all individuals to thrive while remaining rooted in who they are and where they come from.

7. Opportunities to Reflect and Celebrate Growth

- <u>Journaling or reflection</u>: Students can track progress, identify coping strategies, and recognize personal growth.

- <u>Celebrating effort and small wins</u>: Recognizing perseverance reinforces setbacks are temporary and solvable.

- <u>Storytelling and modeling</u>: Sharing examples of overcoming challenges teaches resilience by example.

FACING AND OVERCOMING ADVERSITY

I wish that every student would take the time to reflect on their journey, regardless of what grade level. Reflection allows us to recognize how far we've come, while celebration affirms that our effort mattered. When individuals pause to reflect on progress—both big and small—they gain clarity, confidence, and motivation. Celebrating growth reinforces resilience by shifting focus from perfection to progress, from setbacks to lessons learned. Together, reflection and celebration build hope, strengthen self-belief, and encourage continued growth, reminding us that development is a journey worth honoring.

In essence, a classroom fostering resilience is safe, supportive, challenging, and empowering. It balances structure with flexibility, high expectations with nurturing, and guidance with autonomy. Students leave not only academically prepared but also emotionally equipped to navigate life's challenges.

Finally, creating resilient classrooms is essential because they do more than support academic learning. They protect, stabilize, and strengthen students so they can succeed despite adversity.

Below are some key reasons, grounded in both educational practice and resilience research:

1. Students Bring Adversity into the Classroom

Many students arrive carrying:

- trauma
- chronic stress
- instability
- unmet emotional needs

A resilient classroom doesn't ignore this reality—it responds to it. It becomes a place of predictability and safety, which are foundational for learning.

Regulated students learn better.

2. *Learning Cannot Thrive Without Emotional Safety*

When students feel unsafe—emotionally or relationally—their brains shift into survival mode.

Resilient classrooms prioritize:

- trust
- consistency
- respectful relationships

This allows the brain to move from fight-or-flight to engagement and problem-solving.

3. *Resilience Is a Teachable Skill*

Resilience is not a trait students either have or don't have—it is developed.

Resilient classrooms intentionally teach:

- emotional regulation
- problem-solving
- perseverance
- healthy coping strategies

These skills prepare students not only for tests, but for life beyond school.

4. *Resilient Classrooms Reduce Behavioral Issues*

When students feel connected and supported:

- disruptions decrease
- engagement increases
- accountability improves

Behavior shifts from reaction to response, saving instructional time and strengthening classroom culture.

FACING AND OVERCOMING ADVERSITY

5. *Equity Requires Resilience*

Students facing poverty, trauma, or systemic barriers need schools to be protective environments.

Resilient classrooms:

- level the playing field
- reduce the impact of external stressors
- provide access to hope, structure, and support

Chapter 12 – What Resilient Students Do Differently: Profiles, Patterns, and Practices

When we look at students who thrive in the face of challenges, it's not that their lives are easier or their paths are smoother. What sets resilient students apart is what they do when life gets difficult. They experience failure, disappointment, pressure, and adversity just like everyone else—but instead of stopping, they adjust. Instead of giving up, they try again. Resilient students think differently, respond differently, and recover differently. They've learned skills, mindsets, and habits that allow them not just to survive hard moments, but to grow through them. And the powerful truth is this: resilience isn't something you're simply born with—it's something that can be taught, practiced, and strengthened in every student.

It always amazes me to watch resilient students. Whether in the classroom or on the athletic field. Witnessing a resilient 1st grader trying to open their lunchable at lunch time can be both funny and enlightening as they maneuver unwrapping the container which could take time. After a few minutes of struggle the resilient student seeks help from a lunch aide who will in turn show them the best way to open the package. This is classic resilient behavior at best all because they recognize the need for help when struggling.

Then there's the non-resilient 10th grade female who doesn't make the football cheerleading team. She storms out of the gym after not seeing her name posted on the wall as being selected. A teacher stops the student to discuss what has caused her to be angry. The student begins, with elevated voice, "I hate coach Smith because she plays favorites," "I'm better than many of the girls who tried out and where selected." When the teacher asked what the student would do next, the student shared, "Nothing." The better response would have been, "I will seek help to get better, and try again next year."

In every K–12 classroom, students respond to challenges in various ways. Some students encounter setbacks and find ways to adapt, recover, and keep moving forward, while others become overwhelmed, discouraged, or disengaged when difficulties arise. These differences are often described in terms of resilience. Resilient students are not those who avoid adversity, but those who have developed the skills, supports, and beliefs needed to navigate it. In contrast, non-resilient students may struggle not because they lack ability or motivation, but because they lack protective factors such as consistent relationships, emotional regulation skills, or a sense of hope. Understanding this distinction shifts the focus from "What is wrong with the student?" to "What does this student need to thrive?"

When tackling what resilient students do differently, I like to begin with delineating some of the differences between the resilient and the non-resilient student. Let's first look at the resilient student, then the non-resilient student.

Resilient Students

Resilient students are not defined by the absence of struggle, but by how they respond when struggle appears. What they do differently reflects learned skills, supportive relationships, and an internal sense of agency.

In contrast to students who become stuck by adversity, resilient students tend to respond in the following ways:

They interpret challenges differently.

Resilient students view setbacks as temporary and specific rather than permanent or personal. A poor grade, peer conflict, or disciplinary moment is seen as something to work through, not as a verdict on their worth or ability.

They regulate emotions instead of reacting impulsively

Rather than being controlled by frustration, fear, or anger, resilient students use coping strategies—such as pausing, naming emotions, or seeking support—to regain emotional balance and make thoughtful choices.

They persist and adjust.

When a strategy fails, resilient students are more likely to try a different approach instead of giving up. Persistence is paired with flexibility, allowing them to adapt rather than disengage.

They seek connection and support.

Resilient students recognize when they need help and are willing to reach out to trusted adults or peers. Strong relationships act as a buffer against stress and reinforce a sense of safety and belonging.

They maintain a sense of hope and purpose.

Even in difficult circumstances, resilient students believe their efforts matter and that improvement is possible. This forward-looking mindset fuels motivation and protects against hopelessness.

They take responsibility without self-blame.

Resilient students can acknowledge mistakes and learn from them without internalizing shame. Accountability becomes a pathway to growth rather than a source of defeat.

For educators, the critical takeaway is that these behaviors are taught, modeled, and reinforced. Resilience grows when schools intentionally create environments that combine high expectations with consistent support, emotional skill-building, and meaningful relationships.

Non-Resilient Students

Student's that lack resiliency often struggles to recover from setbacks and may feel overwhelmed by challenges. When difficulties arise, they may:

- View failure as a reflection of their worth or ability
- Become easily discouraged and give up quickly
- Struggle to regulate emotions such as frustration, anger, or anxiety
- Avoid challenges or disengage from learning
- Rely on negative coping behaviors or withdraw socially
- Have limited access to supportive relationships or lack trust in adults
- Feel hopeless or powerless when facing adversity

These responses are often rooted not in unwillingness, but in unmet needs—such as a lack of emotional skills, consistent support, or safe environments.

For educators, the critical takeaway is that these behaviors are taught, modeled, and reinforced. Resilience grows when schools intentionally create environments that combine high expectations with consistent support, emotional skill-building, and meaningful relationships.

Chapter 13 – Rewriting the Story: Teaching Students to Challenge False Narratives

Resilience is not only about "weathering and recovering," from adversity but also learning to recognize and rewrite the stories students believe about themselves. Many students carry internal narratives such as "I'm a failure," "I'll never succeed," "Failure is normal in my family," or "My past defines me." These false narratives inevitably shape behavior, limit effort, limit confidence, and suffocate potential. If we want resilient students, we must equip and encourage them to challenge unhealthy beliefs and replace them with truthful, empowering mindsets.

Why the Stories Student's Tell Themselves Matter

The brain naturally seeks meaning; when students don't understand why something happened, they create a story. Trauma, repeated failure, criticism, and comparison all feed negative internal scripts. Over time, these stories become lenses through which students interpret life. A resilient student isn't one without pain or difficulty. A resilient student is one who learns to question the story instead of accepting it as truth.

False narratives matter to resilience because the stories we tell ourselves shape who we believe we are. When students learn to turn difficult experiences into meaningful stories of growth rather than defeat, they build strength, understanding, and emotional coping skills. With the guidance of caring adults, children can learn to question untrue or unhelpful assumptions—about themselves, others, or situations—and reframe them into healthier, more accurate perspectives. This ability to challenge negative "made-up" stories and create more empowering ones is a powerful social-emotional skill and a core part of developing resilience.

Helping Students Name the Narrative

A false narrative must be challenged before it can be changed. Students must learn to first identify the false narrative. Educators can help students slow down and notice what they are saying to themselves when they struggle.

- "How can I help you reframe what you said about things not going your way?"
- "What conclusion have you reached about this story?"
- "If you could rename this story and give it a title, what would it be?"

Helping students name the narrative brings it out of the shadows and into the light where it can be examined with curiosity rather than shame.

Strengthening Students Ability to Ask Thoughtful Questions

Resilient students, with help from positive adults, learn to question their thoughts instead of aimlessly trusting them. It is critical that we teach students to ask leading resilience-building questions:

- Is there truth to this story, or am I feeling a certain way at the moment?
- What evidence supports this thought, and what evidence challenges it?
- Is my problem temporary or permanent?

- What would I say if my friend was experiencing this?
- Should I consider looking at this another way?

These questions retrain the brain to evaluate rather than emotionally react. Students begin to understand that thoughts are not facts—and that they have the power to reframe.

Replacing Harmful Narratives with Healthier Truths

Challenging a false narrative doesn't stop at identifying it; as the next step is to abrogate and substitute it with a healthier, realistic, and empowering narrative. We are not teaching false positivity. We are teaching grounded truth.

False Narrative: "I'm not good at History."

Resilient Narrative: "History is challenging, but with tutoring I can get better."

False Narrative: "I'm a nobody at this school."

Resilient Narrative: "It feels lonely right now, but getting connected with the book club will help me feel good about being here."

False Narrative: "I failed, so failure is how it will continue to be."

Resilient Narrative: "Failure is not the end of my story. I must keep writing my story, one chapter at a time."

This shift helps students view challenges as opportunities rather than verdicts.

Cultivating Classroom Climates That Correct Distorted Narratives

Students are more likely to rewrite harmful beliefs when they are surrounded by educators who speak life, encourage possibility, and focus on truth.

- Normalize struggle. Talk transparently about mistakes, setbacks, and growth.
- Encourage celebration when progress is achieved, not perfection.
- Model rewriting narratives. Let students hear you say, "I've had my struggles but this is how I was able to overcame."
- Challenge deficit language. When students say "I can't," respond with "Believe in yourself."
- Use stories of resilience such as Literature, history, and lived experiences as mirrors of hope.

The environment we create either reinforces false narratives or helps dismantle them.

Teaching Emotional Literacy Alongside Narrative Awareness

Students will struggle to change false narratives when they do not understand what they feel. Their inability to name their emotions like fear, shame, disappointment, frustration reduces their power. When students understand their emotional responses, they can more accurately challenge the story attached to them.

"I'm not stupid. I'm frustrated."

"I'm not angry, I am overwhelmed."

"I'm not incapable. I'm discouraged."

Language gives students a sense of control.

The Role of Caring Adults

Students rarely challenge false narratives on their own. They need caring adults who:

FACING AND OVERCOMING ADVERSITY

- See beyond behavior
- Speak to potential rather than performance
- Offer consistent encouragement
- Believe in students even when students don't believe in themselves

When students borrow an adult's belief long enough, it often becomes their own.

The Result: A Resilient Identity

When students learn to challenge false narratives, they reshape their identity and begin an upward trajectory towards destiny. They move from:

- Helplessness to agency
- Shame to self-compassion
- Limitation to possibility
- Survival to growth

Resilience grows not simply because life becomes easier, but because students learn to think differently about themselves and their circumstances. Teaching students to challenge false narratives is not just a skill—it is a gift that shapes who they become.

Chapter 14 – Growth Mindset and How It Influences Resilience

Resilient students are not immune to challenges. Many students experience setbacks, disappointment, and failure just like everyone else. It is not unusual to see students walking through the halls of Youngstown City School District who are in crisis, coming out of crisis, or getting ready to go into a crisis. Challenges are the norm for many of our students but what sets them apart is the will, determination, and desire to keep going when they want to give up. What sets them apart is not circumstance, but how they interpret and respond to challenges. One of the most powerful ways to foster this perspective is through cultivating a growth mindset.

Understanding Growth Mindset

The concept of growth mindset comes from psychologist Carol Dweck. It refers to the belief that intelligence, abilities, and skills are not fixed traits, but qualities that can develop through effort, strategies, and persistence. Dr. Dweck says, "A growth mindset is about believing people can develop their abilities" (Dweck, 2006). Dr. Dweck, further purports that, "A fixed mindset is the belief that abilities are innate and unchangeable" (Dweck, 2006).

Students with a growth mindset see challenges as opportunities to learn rather than threats to their identity. They embrace struggle, value effort, and understand that failure is part of the learning process. In contrast, students with a fixed mindset often avoid challenges, give up easily, and interpret mistakes as a reflection of their inherent ability.

Key ideas of a growth mindset

- Mistakes are opportunities to learn, not signs of failure.
- Effort is valuable, not embarrassing.
- Feedback helps improvement rather than feeling like criticism.
- "I can't do this... yet" replaces "I can't do this."

Example:

A student who fails a spelling test with a growth mindset says, "My score was not good, but I can do better."

Key Ideas of a fixed mindset

- Works to prove intelligence or talent.
- Avoids challenges for fear of failure.
- Avoids hard labor.
- Treats criticism as an attack.

Example:

A student who fails a spelling test with a fixed mindset thinks, "I'm just bad at spelling."

The Link Between Growth Mindset and Resilience

Growth mindset and resilience are closely intertwined. Here's why:

1. Persistence Through Setbacks

A growth-oriented student views failure as a temporary obstacle, not a permanent judgment. This perspective allows them to try again, problem-solve, and adapt strategies—core elements of resilience.

2. *Adaptive Coping Strategies*

Students with a growth mindset are more likely to seek help, experiment with different approaches, and reflect on what went wrong. They see challenges as informational, not personal, which reduces stress and fosters emotional regulation.

3. *Positive Self-Talk and Narrative Reframing*

Growth-minded students often engage in self-encouraging dialogue, such as:

- "I haven't mastered this yet."
- "Mistakes help me learn."
- "Effort will pay off over time."

This internal reframing strengthens resilience by replacing self-defeating thoughts with constructive, motivating ones.

4. *Enhanced Motivation and Engagement*

Believing that improvement is possible fuels motivation and investment in learning, even when tasks are difficult. Students become resilient not because they never fail, but because they see value in learning and growth.

Practical Strategies to Foster a Growth Mindset

1. *Model Growth Mindset as an Educator*

- Share personal challenges and learning journeys
- Use language that emphasizes effort and learning over innate talent
- Normalize struggle as part of the growth process

2. *Reframe Failure and Setbacks*

Encourage statements like:

- "What can I learn from this?"
- "This attempt is a step toward mastery."
- Use reflective prompts to help students identify lessons from mistakes

3. Celebrate Effort and Process

- Highlight persistence, strategy use, and progress rather than only grades or outcomes
- Reinforce that effort is a skill to cultivate, not a sign of weakness

4. Teach Goal-Setting and Incremental Steps

- Help students break larger challenges into achievable steps
- Track progress over time to visualize improvement
- Encourage personal reflection on growth, not comparison with others

5. Provide Feedback That Promotes Growth

- Focus on specific strategies and behaviors rather than labeling the student
- Example: "Your revision shows strong persistence and critical thinking" instead of "You're smart"

Growth Mindset Activities for the Classroom

- Reflection Journals: Students write about a recent challenge and identify what they learned.
- Success Stories: Share real-life or historical examples of individuals who succeeded through persistence.

- Mindset Language Practice: Teach students to rephrase "I can't do this" with "I can't do this yet."
- Peer Feedback Circles: Encourage constructive, growth-oriented feedback on assignments or projects.

Finally, growth mindset is more than a motivational phrase—it is a practical, evidence-based approach to nurturing resilience in students. By helping children believe in the potential to grow, we equip them to face setbacks, embrace challenges, and persist when life gets difficult. A growth mindset does not eliminate adversity, but it transforms how students respond to it, turning obstacles into opportunities for learning, growth, and stronger resilience.

Chapter 15 – Hope: Teaching Students to See Possibility

In this chapter, I will spend time communicating how hope shared can transform students' lives. Hope is one of the most powerful protective factors a student can possess. For students navigating adversity (poverty, instability, trauma, academic struggle, or fractured relationships) hope becomes the mental and emotional engine that allows them to imagine a life beyond their current circumstances. Hope doesn't erase hardship, but it reframes it. It tells students, "Your story isn't finished yet," and that belief alone begins to build the foundation of resilience.

Hope is one of the most powerful forces that shapes how individuals confront and overcome adversity. It does not erase challenges, but it transforms the way people experience them. When hope is present, adversity is no longer viewed as a permanent or defining barrier; instead, it becomes a moment in time that can be navigated, learned from, and ultimately overcome.

Hope fuels perseverance by reminding individuals that their efforts matter and that a positive outcome is still possible, even when the path is uncertain. It strengthens problem-solving by opening the mind to new strategies, supportive relationships, and creative solutions. Emotionally, hope serves as a protective buffer, reducing the weight of fear, discouragement, and despair. In many ways, hope becomes both an anchor and a compass—steadying people during the storm while guiding them toward a future brighter than their present circumstances.

Hope expands a student's sense of possibility. Adversity often narrows a child's vision until all they can see is the problem in front of them. Hope widens that vision, helping them recognize that new options, new support, and new outcomes are still within reach. When students believe that a better tomorrow is possible, they become more willing to try, to practice, to ask for help, and to stay engaged even when success feels slow. Hope fuels persistence.

Hope also strengthens a student's identity. When caring adults (teachers, counselors, mentors) speak life into children, they help them see themselves as capable, worthy, and resilient. That shift in self-perception is transformative. A student who believes "I can grow" approaches challenges with more confidence and less fear. Hope empowers them to reinterpret adversity as a temporary obstacle rather than a permanent limitation.

Equally important, hope connects students to others. It grows in relationships where belonging, encouragement, and trust are present. When a student feels supported, they learn that they do not have to face adversity alone. This sense of connection is essential for resilience because it provides stability, accountability, and emotional safety which are elements that buffer the impact of stress.

Ultimately, hope is the spark that activates resilience. It gives students the courage to move forward, the strength to endure difficulty, and the vision to see beyond the moment. Hope transforms adversity into an opportunity for growth, shaping students into young people who understand their own power, who can persevere through struggle, and rise stronger on the other side.

What is Hope? How can Hope play a major role in the lives of the children in your classrooms that you work with day in and day out? Hope can mean a lot of things to different people, though no matter how you frame it or experience it, hope is a vital aspect of our experience as human beings. Hope is always about the future. The term hope has been defined as, "Hope is the sum of the mental willpower and waypower that you have for your goals" (Snyder, 1994, p. 5). Hope can be further understood as a positive motivational state that is fueled by being positively motivated (agency) and a road map (pathways) to reach a goal.

Dr. Lopez, in his book "Making Hope Happen," shares four core prerequisites for hope that are powerful and can be useful for our students today. He says "The future will be better than the present," "I have the power to make it so," "There are many paths to my goal," "None of them is free of obstacles" (Lopez, 2013, pp. 18-19).

I define hope as, "The confident expectation of a desired outcome, based upon an inward conviction." This definition is rooted in my spiritual belief based upon Hebrews 11:1, "Now faith is the substance of things hoped for, the evidence of things not seen."

It is my hope to provide you with a perspective and practical application of hope necessary to change the narrative of lives enveloped by the despair of adversity and trauma.

- One reality that children who have suffered from adversity and traumatic experiences have in common is that they're grasping for something that will ignite hope.
- Many are hoping for change, for the despair to stop, that things will get better. Some are hoping that the turbulence, trials and tribulation will cease, that relief will manifest giving them relief/peace.

Many students, regardless of their geographic location, household make-up, and economic status face adversity. Stress, anxiety, and depression are but a few challenges which severely impact their academic achievement and healthy development. There are other social conditions, no doubt, that breed a sense of meaningless and hopelessness, which also impact their daily functioning. As result of these intractable challenges, students and those who support them, including teachers, their families, and community institutions, struggle to engage them in meaningful ways.

I must speak truth to power as the options to help our students, at times, seem few and far in between. This however, doesn't mean we must give in to the notion there's nothing else we can do to help students address and overcome their adversities. We must continue to build upon the strategies mentioned in the previous chapter to fill our "Hope Toolbox," with tools that enable us to restore hope and well-being. We can start by asking probing questions such as How do I as a teacher effectively respond to a student (s) experiencing hopelessness in ways that restore dignity, hope, and possibility? How can the responses given cause me to pursue action? What are the elements that will lead to a transformative culture and climate in my school/classroom?

I purport to you that students need a double dose of hope when they arrive in your classrooms as they may have come to school hungry, not having adequate rest due to police and ambulance sirens sounding off through the night, then having to deal with gang violence on the way home from school. Maybe, your student (s) have come in having the adversity of dealing with parents in the midst of divorce. Could it be your student (s) are facing peer pressure that's mentally and emotionally debilitating? Have you been approached by a student who informs you that they've considered, because of life's circumstances, suicide? These aforementioned situations and circumstances are but a few of the reasons helping students see the power of hope and possibility is absolutely necessary.

FACING AND OVERCOMING ADVERSITY

My grandmother, who transitioned while I was an undergraduate in college, would always encourage me. I didn't realize at that time she was teaching me to be hopeful. She would ask me to repeat saying, "I think I can, I think I can." I often remembered her words of affirmation while competing as a track and field athlete. Her words resonated with me in times of fatigue, stress, and difficulty. Saying, I think I can would prove to be the mental energy I needed to stay on schedule to meet my goals. Many of our scholars would benefit from hearing words of hope spoken to them from educators on a daily basis. The words "I think I can," should be a part of every child's vocabulary, to allow hope to usher them to a time and space of achievement, success and greatness. Christopher Reeve said, "Once you choose hope, anything's possible."

I absolutely love Bobby McFerrin's song "Don't Worry, Be Happy," and Pharrell's song, "Happy." I realize these songs are not a miraculous fix to the perplexity of adversity and traumatic events that happens in students' lives however, I do believe they convey a sense of "Collective Possibility." It is about the intentional act of gathering hope, options, and alternative pathways so that resilience can grow in the face of adversity. When students are overwhelmed or discouraged, their brain narrows its vision. Collecting possibility widens their vision again. It helps students believe, "Maybe there's another way," "Maybe things can improve." This is about curated hope.

Educators can engage in what I'm calling "Collective Possibilities." As educators, you can say, "Notice what is working," "Help students name past successes," "Reframe challenges as learning opportunities." We must build a mindset of hope by paying attention to opportunities, strengths, and potential solutions rather than the obstacles before us.

One of the most compelling illustrations of resilience can be found in the true story portrayed in movie "The Boys in the Boat." The University of Washington rowing team, composed primarily of working-class young men, rose from obscurity to Olympic victory not because they were the strongest or came from privilege, but because they learned to transform adversity into collective strength. Their journey mirrors the same resilience we strive to cultivate in K–12 students—resilience shaped by struggle, strengthened through connection, and sustained by purpose.

The story focuses on Joe Rantz, a young man who experienced profound hardship long before he ever stepped into a boat. Abandonment, poverty, and emotional instability could have defined his trajectory. Instead, rowing became a place where adversity was not a barrier but a catalyst. In the rhythm of the oars and the discipline of daily training, Joe discovered that resilience is not merely surviving difficulty but finding a way to grow through it. His persistence reflects the reality many students face and it's in the adversity that their greatest challenges often become the very ground on which their resilience is built.

The true power of the story emerges when the focus shifts from individual grit to collective resilience. What set the team apart was not physical dominance but their ability to move as one. Eight individuals synchronizing their effort, breath, and trust (A school district must collectively work together). Success demanded communication, vulnerability, and a willingness to sacrifice personal glory for shared purpose. This mirrors the classroom, where students flourish when they experience belonging, connection, and supportive relationships. Just as the crew's boat glided only when their rhythms were aligned, students thrive when the school environment is cohesive, collaborative, and grounded in mutual respect.

FACING AND OVERCOMING ADVERSITY

The team's triumph reminds educators that resilience is not only taught but modeled, nurtured, and reinforced through community. Their coaches served as mentors, encouragers, and stabilizers, helping the boys see beyond their circumstances. Likewise, educators become the steady voice guiding students toward hope when life feels uncertain. The victory at the 1936 Olympics was not simply an athletic achievement; it was evidence of what becomes possible when young people are given belief, structure, and the opportunity to rise. Ultimately, The Boys in the Boat teaches that resilience is both personal and communal. It is forged in adversity but strengthened in connection. Those young rowers learned to pull together toward a destination bigger than themselves. Our students must learn to navigate life's waters with confidence when surrounded by adults and peers who row beside them.

So, what is the hope we must give our students? It is the hope that encourages, inspires, and walks with them in their times of darkness. There will be times when life is dark, when our students are asking the question, "will I be able to overcome what I'm going through?" It is in the dark that hope allows you and I and the children we work with to see the light ahead. This is the hope we must give to our children.

Hope enables our children to say I can, I will, I must work past my situation, believing its but another transition I have to go through, climb out of, and work through. We must encourage our children to believe another day will occur, the sun will shine again, that hope allows them to see past the fog of their circumstances, catching the horizon of their future.

Hope fuels our children to get up in the morning, desiring to walk into the halls of academia, grinding day in and day out to maximize their educational potential. Hope says yes, I can, I may be down but not out, I'm more than a conqueror! Hope is the reminder of how good things can be when you reach down into the inner most part of your being past the present moment of pain, disappointment and failure to say, "my future will be better than my past."

Why Hope

It is my belief that the greatest challenge facing America today is the increasing level of hopelessness that is growing, especially in our schools. It is a hopelessness that is fueled by inequality, injustice, disparity and isolation. It is a hopelessness that we must address even in our schools. How can we begin, where do we begin, and why should we begin to embrace the challenge of practicing hope in our districts, buildings, and classrooms? When I consider hope, I do so because:

- Hope heals. Because hope can transform a traumatized child. Hope is the lifeblood of resilience.
- Hope is having that inner capacity which has been nurtured and fully developed to the point of conviction. True hope is that inner conviction and determination that will cause you to keep moving forward even while the darkness shields your eyes from the light that everything inside tells you is just around the bend.
- Hope, is having that internal capacity to see no obstacle or challenge as being greater than you.
- Hope builds resilience. True hope can look any momentary setback in the eyes and say with conviction…I will!!

Fostering hope in your students:

As educators, parents, and coaches we have the responsibility to teach and instill hope in the students we are entrusted with. Why? Because hope should be an essential ingredient in the development of children. It is a tool that ultimately allows our students to navigate life's challenges. With the news, social media, and every day real-life situations enveloping young people with despair, tragedy, and death, we must make every effort to find ways to share positivity, joy, and hope. Here are a few ways to impact students with hope:

1. Visually exhibit an attitude of hope
2. Allow your students to take ownership over their accomplishments
3. Remind your students those challenges are life lessons
4. Verbalize your students potential and effort

I close this chapter with some powerful but practical strategies to help k-12 students develop hope and see possibility:

1. Teach a "Possibility Mindset" Through Language

Students learn possibility through the word's adults use.

Replace "I can't" with "I can't yet."

Use sentence starters such as:

- "What's another way we could approach this?"
- "What might be possible if…?"
- "What would success look like for you?"

Why it works: Language shifts the brain toward creative, expansive thinking instead of limitation.

2. Strengthen Students' Sense of Personal Agency

Give students structured opportunities to make real choices:

- Let them select project topics.
- Allow choice in learning pathways.
- Invite them to co-create classroom norms.

Why it works: Agency fuels hope. When students feel their actions influence outcomes, they can imagine new futures.

3. Model "Possibility Thinking" as an Educator

Students watch what teachers believe more than what they say.

- Share stories of your own challenges and how you discovered options.
- Verbalize your thinking when you hit a tough moment:
- "This didn't work—we need another strategy. Let's brainstorm."

Why it works: Your transparency teaches them that solutions exist—even when they are not immediate.

4. Use Future-Oriented Visualization Activities

Have students:

- Write letters to their future selves.
- Map out "one-year goals," "one-month goals," and "one-week actions."
- Draw a "future version" of themselves with strengths and achievements.

Why it works: Visualization activates hope pathways and helps students test-drive possibility.

5. Celebrate Progress, Not Perfection

Praise:

- Effort
- Creativity
- Strategy use
- Courage to try new things

FACING AND OVERCOMING ADVERSITY

Why it works: Students learn that growth is possible even when outcomes are not perfect.

6. Teach Students to Reframe Adversity

Introduce reframing questions:

- "What is this challenge trying to teach me?"
- "What strength am I using right now?"
- "How might this help me in the future?"

Why it works: Reframing builds resilience by turning setbacks into stepping stones.

7. Surround Students with "Possibility Examples"

Use:

- Stories of individuals who overcame adversity.
- Classroom displays highlighting student achievements.
- Quick case studies of young innovators, survivors, creators, and changemakers.

Why it works: Representation builds belief.

8. Incorporate Collaborative Problem-Solving

Provide group tasks that require creativity:

- Build challenges
- Open-ended projects
- Design thinking lessons

Ask:

- "How many solutions can your group come up with?"

Why it works: Multiple approaches teach students that there is rarely only one way forward.

9. *Teach Students to Name Their Strengths*

Use strengths assessments or simple sentence frames:

- "One strength I see in myself is…"
- "A strength others notice in me is…"

Why it works: Students who know what they bring to the table can imagine new opportunities.

10. *Replace "What's wrong?" with "What's possible?"*

At moments of frustration, teach a simple pivot:

- Instead of asking "What's the problem?" ask:
- "What's possible right now?"
- "What's one small next step you can take?"

Why it works: Students learn to shift from problem-focus to possibility-focus.

I conclude this chapter with words from Dr. Lopez who says, "Hope matters," "Hope is a choice," "Hope can be learned," "Hope can be shared with others" (Lopez, 2013, p. 13).

"In fact, hope is best gained after defeat and failure, because then inner strength and toughness is produced." (Fritz Knapp, May 10, 2020).

Chapter 16 – From Struggle to Strength: How Students Grow Beyond Adversity

Adversity is what we experience when life gets hard, unfair, overwhelming, or uncertain. Also, adversity becomes a place where resilience can be developed. Adversity is not the end of a student's story; for many, it becomes the moment their story begins to change. Students do not simply "bounce back" from hardship—they grow forward when the right supports, environments, and personal strengths converge. Thriving beyond adversity is not accidental; it is the result of connection, skill building, hope, and intentional guidance.

There are many types of adversity students will face. There is personal adversity such as family illness, grief from death, and self-doubt. Social adversity can manifest in ways such as bullying, exclusion, even identify challenges. The environment plays a role in adversity. Students who come from impoverished backgrounds, unsafe neighborhoods, and unstable living conditions are impacted. Then there are academic adversities like learning gaps, pressure to achieve, and discouragement. Traumatic adversity can rear its ugly head by way of abuse, violence, and chronic stress.

What I believe, have seen, and stand on is that adversity does not automatically break our students. Yes, it tests, shapes, and with the right support strengthens them. It becomes a defining place where resilience character, and perseverance are formed.

Thriving Begins with Connection

The most consistent predictor of thriving after adversity is a caring relationship with a trustworthy adult.

Students flourish when someone consistently communicates:

- You matter.
- You are capable.
- You are not alone.

The aforementioned affirmations are important to students who are becoming resilient. As they, not only build connection, but enable students to hear from those they are connected with and believe to be an integral part of their lives.

Affirmation is more than kind words—it is an intentional act of speaking truth, value, and possibility into someone's life. For students facing pressure, doubt, or adversity, affirmation becomes a stabilizing force that shapes identity, confidence, and hope. When caring adults communicate, "I see you. I believe in you. You are capable of greatness," affirmation interrupts negative self-talk, counters shame-based narratives, and replaces fear with belief.

Affirmation strengthens the brain's emotional pathways connected to confidence and perseverance. It helps students internalize messages of worth and ability, shifting their mindset from "I can't" to "I can try" and eventually to "I can succeed." Consistent, authentic affirmation builds resilience because it reminds students that failure is not final, mistakes are not identity, and struggle is not a measure of their worth. Over time, affirmed students develop stronger self-regulation, clearer purpose, and a deeper sense of belonging

Teachers, counselors, parents, mentors, and coaches become anchors during turbulent seasons. These relationships stabilize emotions, restore confidence, and remind students that they are valued beyond their circumstances. Belonging is not optional—it is protective.

Mindset Transforms Struggle into Growth

Students thrive when they develop a resilient mindset—the belief that challenges can shape, not shatter, their future.

They learn to reinterpret adversity:

- Setbacks become temporary.
- Failure becomes feedback.
- Struggle becomes strength-building.

This mindset shifts students from helplessness to agency. Instead of asking, "Why is this happening to me?" they begin to ask, "What can I learn from what I'm going through? How can I grow from what I've experienced?" The way students think about adversity determines how they respond to it. The connection and affirmation that students receive from any adult is laudable. Affirmation takes the connection further. When adults speak truthful, specific encouragement into a student's life, it shapes identify and mindset.

Ultimately, it is laudable because it is both morally right and educationally powerful. It honors student's humanity while equipping them with courage, resilience, and self-worth. Connection and affirmation do not simply help students feel good, it helps them become stronger, healthier, and more capable of reaching their maximum potential.

Emotional Regulation Builds Internal Strength

Thriving students learn how to manage overwhelming feelings. They are taught how to name emotions, understand what they are experiencing, and use healthy coping strategies—breathing techniques, movement, reflection, journaling, conversation, or prayer. Emotional awareness does not erase adversity, but it strengthens the nervous system and improves focus, behavior, and decision-making. Students who can regulate emotions are better equipped to persist academically and socially.

Imagine a middle school student named Jason. During class, he receives a lower grade on an assignment he worked hard on. He feels frustrated and disappointed—his heart beats faster, his face feels warm, and negative thoughts begin to swirl. But instead of reacting impulsively, Jordan practices skills he has learned.

He takes a slow breath to calm his body. He quietly reminds himself, "I'm upset right now, but I can handle this." Instead of slamming his notebook or shutting down, he asks to speak with his teacher after class. When they talk, Jordan expresses his feelings respectfully: "I was really disappointed with my grade. Can you help me understand what I need to improve?" Together, they review his work, identify ways to grow, and he leaves with a plan rather than a meltdown. It is clear that Jason, because of being able to regulate his emotions, exhibits internal strength. Jason's internal strength will serve him, not only in the classroom, but in every facet of his life.

Purpose Fuels Persistence

Students who thrive beyond adversity have a reason to keep going. Purpose may come from faith, family, mentors, personal goals, or a vision of the future. Purpose gives pain meaning and transforms endurance into determination. Hope becomes a powerful protective factor—not blind optimism, but a grounded belief that effort matters, tomorrow can be better, and they have a role in shaping it.

Over the course of many years in education, I've seen many students, regardless of their grade, wondering about aimlessly. The adversities of life have affected them and they have not considered their life purpose (who they want to become, where they want to go, how to get where they want to go). The phrase "Without vision, people perish" speaks to what happens when individuals live without direction, meaning, or a sense of where their lives are headed. When applied to students, it paints a powerful picture: students who live without purpose often do not physically perish, but they can emotionally, academically, and motivationally diminish. Without vision, they <u>drift</u> rather than <u>drive</u>. They may disengage from school, stop believing their effort matters, and lose hope that their future can be meaningful. A lack of purpose leads to apathy, poor decision-making, and vulnerability to negative influences because nothing compelling is pulling them forward.

Purpose, on the other hand, gives students something to reach toward. It fuels motivation, strengthens resilience, and helps them endure adversity. When students have a vision for who they can become and why their life matters, they show greater persistence, better emotional health, stronger academic engagement, and deeper hope. Vision anchor's identity and directs behavior. In short, just as people "perish" without vision, students shrivel inwardly without purpose—but with it, they come <u>alive</u>, <u>strive</u>, and <u>thrive.</u>

Skill Development Turns Hope into Capacity

Thriving is not only emotional; it is practical. Students need opportunities to develop:

- problem-solving
- self-discipline
- communication
- academic competence
- perseverance

Success—no matter how small—creates momentum. Each accomplishment strengthens identity and reinforces a powerful internal message: "I can do hard things." In other words, hope is the motivation, and skill development is the mechanism that allows motivation to translate into achievement. For example, a student may hope to graduate or succeed in a sport or art form, but only by practicing, learning strategies, and applying effort does that hope become actual progress.

Skill development transforms potential energy (hope) into kinetic energy (capable action), enabling students not just to dream about the future, but to actively shape it.

Supportive Schools Help Students Rise

Students thrive when schools intentionally create environments that support resilience. Resilient schools:

- provide psychological safety
- pair high expectations with high support
- foster inclusivity and belonging
- empower student voice and agency
- teach social and emotional skills

Systems either crush resilience or cultivate it. When schools choose empathy, structure, compassion, and high standards, students gain the conditions they need to rise. A critical question for every educator, administrator, and stakeholder is: "Is my school a supportive school that helps students rise?" Supportive schools do more than deliver curriculum—they create environments where students feel seen, valued, and capable. They provide structure without rigidity, high expectations paired with high support, and opportunities for students to learn, grow, and recover from setbacks.

Asking this question forces us, as educators, to examine whether our school actively cultivates resilience or merely reacts to problems. Are students encouraged to take risks and learn from failure? Do they have trusted adults who guide, affirm, and challenge them? Are social-emotional needs prioritized alongside academics?

Rewriting the Narrative

Ultimately, thriving beyond adversity is about story.

Students begin to rewrite internal narratives from:

- "I'm broken" → "I am becoming stronger."
- "I can't change my future" → "I have influence and possibility."
- "This defines me" → "This refines me."

When students learn to rewrite their story, they move from seeing themselves as victims of circumstance to authors of their future. Every student has a story—but not every student has been taught that they can rewrite it. The narratives students tell themselves about who they are, what they are capable of, and what their future holds can either limit them or set them free. When students begin to replace false or limiting beliefs with truths about their effort, growth, and potential, transformation begins. They can say, "Our past may have shaped us, but it does not have to define us."

Rewriting a narrative doesn't erase challenges or mistakes—it reframes them. A student who once thought, "I'll never succeed," can learn to say, "I am learning, growing, and capable of more than I imagined." With guidance, affirmation, and resilience-building strategies, students can shift from feeling powerless to feeling empowered, turning setbacks into lessons and hope into action.

Chapter 17 – The Need for Resilience-Based Interventions for Students

Student's today navigate an increasingly complex world marked by academic pressure, family stressors, social comparison, trauma exposure, community violence, and ongoing uncertainty. These adversities do not impact all students equally; those affected by poverty, discrimination, unstable home environments, or chronic stress are disproportionately impacted. Without intentional support, many young people begin to internalize failure, develop negative identity narratives, disengage from school, and experience emotional and behavioral challenges that hinder learning.

Resilience-based interventions are essential because they move beyond simply reacting to student problems and instead proactively build the internal strengths and external supports students need to thrive. Grounded in resilience science, these interventions help students develop protective factors such as self-regulation, problem-solving, emotional awareness, hope, purpose, and adaptive coping. Equally important, resilience work strengthens relationships with caring adults, fosters belonging, and creates school environments where safety, affirmation, and connection are the norm. When students believe they matter and have the skills to navigate difficulty, they are far more likely to persist, learn, and succeed.

Schools are uniquely positioned to deliver resilience-building supports because students spend a significant portion of their developmental years within school communities. When resilience-based practices are embedded into classrooms, counseling programs, restorative practices, and school culture, they do more than help students "bounce back." They equip students to grow through adversity, build healthy identities, remain emotionally regulated, and pursue meaningful futures. Ultimately, resilience-based interventions are not optional enhancements; they are essential tools for ensuring equity, humanizing education, and supporting student well-being and long-term success.

Without intervention, youth facing significant adversities have a greater likelihood of encountering problems as they navigate their developmental paths (Luthar & Cicchetti, 2000). A key idea is that interventions need to focus on developing assets and resources for those exposed to risk rather than concentrating on risk amelioration (Fegus & Zimmerman, 2005; Luthar & Cicchetti; Yates et al., 2003).

In the past, practitioners focused on documenting predisposing, enabling, and reinforcing factors associated with youth's behavior targeted for change (Fergus & Zimmerman). Typically, deficits are highlighted that predispose, enable, and reinforce negative behaviors; however, a resilience approach emphasizes assets and resources as the center for change. Interventions cutting across behaviors may be the most effective due to the multidimensional nature of resilience. Furthermore, intervention strategies must be tailored to the student's developmental level (Noam & Hermann, 2002).

Moving Beyond a Deficit Lens

Education settings can help move students beyond academic deficit. For too long, education systems have been dominated by deficit thinking. Students struggling behaviorally or academically are labeled "unmotivated," "defiant," or "problem students" (Skiba et al., 2014). This mindset has historically pathologized student behavior, particularly among students from marginalized communities.

Traditional disciplinary responses often punish the symptoms of trauma and stress rather than addressing the root causes. Students are sent away, suspended, or labeled as "behavior problems," when in reality, many are communicating pain they do not yet have the emotional vocabulary to express.

Resilience-based interventions intentionally shift this paradigm. They operate from a strengths-based lens that sees possibility rather than limitation. Instead of asking, "What is wrong with this student?" resilience-centered educators ask, "What has this student experienced, and what support do they need to thrive?" This shift honors student dignity, reinforces belonging, and positions educators as partners in healing rather than being enforcers of compliance.

Research shows that when educators adopt a strength-based, trauma-responsive mindset, student engagement increases, behavior improves, and trust deepens (Brunzell et al., 2018). Resilience-based thinking reframes behavior as communication and invites compassionate intervention rather than exclusion.

Schools serve as primary environments for fostering Resilience Building

Schools are uniquely positioned to foster resilience because they are one of the most stable, predictable environments many children experience. Students spend thousands of hours in classrooms during their formative years. This gives educators an extraordinary opportunity—not only to teach content, but to help shape emotional competence, identity, and coping capacity.

When resilience-based practices are woven into school systems, they do more than respond to crises; they create cultures where:

- connection is prioritized over control

FACING AND OVERCOMING ADVERSITY

- regulation is valued over reaction
- restoration is preferred over punishment
- affirmation replaces shame
- and belonging interrupts isolation

Elementary School Resilience Interventions:

Emotional Regulation - Breathing exercises, mindfulness moments, emotion naming, calm-down corners, feelings charts

Primary Outcomes - Improved self-regulation, reduced meltdowns, emotional awareness

Emotional Literacy - Morning meetings, storybooks on emotions, role-play of feelings, puppetry

Primary Outcomes - Increased understanding of emotions, empathy, expression skills

Social Skills Development - Friendship lessons, sharing practice, turn-taking activities, cooperative games

Primary Outcomes - Stronger peer relationships, fewer conflicts

Predictable Safety & Structure - Visual schedules, consistent routines, positive classroom management

Primary Outcomes - Safety, trust, emotional stability

Growth Mindset Foundations - Encouragement phrases, effort praise, celebrating small wins, learning-from-mistakes activities

Primary Outcomes - Confidence, resilience mindset, perseverance

Family Engagement - Parent communication, family partnership meetings, take-home coping resources

Primary Outcomes - Home–school consistency, support network

Early Restorative Practices - Simple restorative circles, "repair the hurt" conversations, apology and reflection guidance

Primary Outcomes – Accountability with care, relational healing

Middle School Resilience Interventions:

Emotional Regulations & Stress Skills – Coping skills lessons, grounding strategies, journaling, movement breaks

Primary Outcomes – Reduced anxiety, improved impulse control

Identity & Belonging – Advisory programs, student voice groups

Primary Outcomes – Positive identity, peer inclusion, self-worth

Peer Support & Relationships – Peer mentoring, small groups, social skills groups

Primary Outcomes – Decreased isolation, improved connection

Growth Mindset & Academic Resilience – Teaching failure as learning, goal-setting, reflection tools, study resilience strategies

Primary Outcomes – Motivation, persistence, academic engagement

Restorative Justice Practice – Restorative circles, harm repair processes, alternatives to suspension

Primary Outcomes - Reduced conflict, strengthened community trust

High School Resilience Interventions:

Advanced Coping & Stress Management – Cognitive coping skills, stress workshops

Primary Outcomes – Lower anxiety, emotional maturity, healthier coping

FACING AND OVERCOMING ADVERSITY

Purpose, Hope, & Future Orientation – College & career mentoring, goal planning

Primary Outcomes – Motivation, hope, direction, agency

Identify, Voice & Empowerment – Culture identity affirmation, student leadership councils

Primary Outcomes – Empowerment, dignity, positive identity

Life Skills & Resilience Competence – Decision-making lessons, real-world problem solving, resilience curriculum integration

Primary Outcomes – Independence, competence, readiness for adulthood

Restorative & Trauma Response Systems – Restorative conferencing, re-entry support, wraparound services

Primary Outcomes – Reduced suspensions, healing & accountability

Chapter 18 – Profiles in Resilience

The Story of Justus Uwayesu

When we talk about resilience, we are not speaking of convenient inspiration or glossy motivation. We are speaking about a strength born in unthinkable places—where survival itself feels uncertain. Few stories illustrate this truth more clearly than the journey of Justus Uwayesu.

Justus was a child of Rwanda's devastating 1994 genocide, a tragedy that took his parents, fractured his sense of security, and thrust him and his siblings into a life defined by scarcity and fear. With nowhere safe to call home, childhood for Justus did not unfold in classrooms, playgrounds, or places of warmth. Instead, it led him to the outskirts of Kigali—to a garbage dump—where he slept inside the shell of a burned-out car and survived by scavenging.

Yet even in an environment where most young children focus only on getting through the day, Justus carried something remarkable inside him: vision. One day, when humanitarian workers visited the dump searching for children to help, many asked for food, clothing, or money. But when they asked Justus what he wanted most, he did not ask for temporary relief. He answered with uncommon clarity:

"I want to go to school."

That single request—simple yet profound—became the turning point of his life. Education became his doorway out of despair. Once given the opportunity, Justus did not merely attend school; he excelled. He learned languages, rose to the top of his classes, became a student leader, and developed a deep conviction that his success should lift others as well. His determination propelled him to global recognition and ultimately to Harvard University—an outcome almost unimaginable considering where his journey began.

But Justus's story is not simply about personal achievement; it is about transformation with purpose. Rather than distancing himself from his past, he used it as fuel to support others still facing adversity. He helped provide school supplies, financial assistance, and encouragement to vulnerable students, proving that resilience is not only the capacity to rise—it is the willingness to reach back and pull others up.

What Students Learn from Justus

Justus's story teaches students and educators powerful truths:

- Resilience begins with vision. Even when life strips everything else away, the ability to name a future worth striving for is powerful.

- Education is more than academics; it is liberation. Access to learning can reshape identity, restore hope, and redirect destiny.

- Support systems matter. Resilience strengthens when determined young people meet compassionate adults who open doors.

- Purpose deepens resilience. The strongest form of resilience is not merely overcoming hardship—it is transforming hardship into service.

Why This Story Belongs in Our Classrooms

When students encounter Justus's journey, they witness resilience not as theory but as lived reality. They see that hardship does not define destiny. They discover that determination, belief, opportunity, and compassion can change a life—and that they, too, possess the capacity to persevere, choose growth, and impact others.

Justus Uwayesu's life stands as a living testimony: adversity may shape the beginning of one's story, but it does not have to dictate the ending. His journey reminds us that resilience is both a mindset and a mission—a commitment to hope, a dedication to learning, and a promise to ensure that rising is never done alone.

The Story of Ludwig van Beethoven

When we speak of resilience, we often imagine courage in the face of circumstances that challenge physical endurance or emotional strength. But sometimes adversity attack's purpose itself. For the great composer Ludwig van Beethoven, adversity came for the very gift that defined his identity—his hearing.

Beethoven did not begin life with privilege or ease. Raised in a troubled home with an alcoholic father and little stability, his childhood was marked by harsh pressure and emotional turmoil. Music became the place where he found meaning, voice, and a sense of belonging in the world. By his early twenties, Beethoven had earned recognition as one of Europe's most promising young musicians. His gift was undeniable. His future appeared certain.

Then, the unthinkable happened. Beethoven began to lose his hearing. The decline was slow—a faint ringing, muffled conversations, sounds slipping just beyond clarity. But as months turned into years, the loss became permanent and devastating. For a musician, hearing is not a luxury; it is oxygen. Silence threatened not only his career but his identity, dignity, and purpose. In despair, Beethoven withdrew socially, battled depression, and even questioned whether life still had meaning. The world around him grew quieter, colder, and more isolating.

Yet within that darkness, a remarkable decision emerged. Rather than surrender to silence, Beethoven refused to allow his disability to define him. He chose to keep composing, even though he could no longer hear the music he created. He began to "hear" sound internally—through memory, emotional intuition, and imagination. He pressed forward not because the path was easy, but because his calling mattered. His adversities did not weaken his artistry; they deepened it. Out of profound struggle came some of the most emotionally powerful compositions the world has ever known.

Beethoven composed his Ninth Symphony—one of the greatest musical masterpieces in history—while completely deaf. When it debuted, the audience erupted in thunderous applause, but Beethoven could not hear it. He stood facing the orchestra as the hall shook with celebration. Only when a musician gently turned him toward the crowd did he see the overwhelming response. In that moment, applause replaced the silence he had lived with for so long—not in sound, but in recognition of the indomitable spirit behind the music.

What Students Learn from Beethoven

Beethoven's journey teaches students powerful truths about resilience:

- Resilience means refusing to be defined by limitation. Even when something precious is taken away, purpose can remain.

- Adversity can deepen creativity and strength. Hardship does not always shrink our capacity; sometimes it stretches it.

- Persistence is not denial of pain—it is choosing meaning despite it.

- True greatness is not the absence of struggle; it is what rises from within it.

Why His Story Matters for Today's Students

Student's today face emotional challenges, learning struggles, discouragement, trauma, and moments when they feel unheard, unseen, or overwhelmed. Beethoven's story reminds them that even when life alters a dream, it does not erase potential. Resilience does not always mean returning to life as it was; sometimes it means courageously redefining what is possible.

Beethoven's life echoes a profound message: adversity may change the conditions of our journey, but it does not have to silence our purpose. His legacy teaches us that resilience is not only endurance—it is transformation.

The Hidden Figures Story

Resilience is often forged quietly—far from recognition, applause, or public praise. The true story portrayed in the film Hidden Figures reveals resilience lived out in perseverance, brilliance, and dignity by three extraordinary women: Katherine Johnson, Dorothy Vaughan, and Mary Jackson. Their story teaches students that resilience is not only about surviving hardship, but about excelling in the face of injustice and opening doors for others to follow.

Set during the early days of NASA's space program, these three African American women worked as mathematicians and engineers at a time when both racial segregation and gender discrimination shaped daily life. They were often excluded from meetings, denied opportunities, and forced to work harder simply to be seen as equal. Yet they refused to allow discrimination to define their worth or limit their contributions.

Katherine Johnson demonstrated intellectual resilience. Her extraordinary mathematical ability helped calculate flight trajectories critical to America's space missions, including John Glenn's historic orbit of Earth. Even when her work was questioned or dismissed because of her race or gender, Katherine stood firm in confidence, competence, and quiet determination. Her resilience was rooted in excellence.

Dorothy Vaughan embodied leadership resilience. When she realized her department was being phased out due to technological changes, she did not resist progress—she mastered it. Dorothy taught herself and her team computer programming, ensuring their relevance and securing future opportunities not only for herself, but for the women she led. Her resilience lifted others as she rose.

Mary Jackson modeled advocacy resilience. With dreams of becoming an engineer, Mary faced legal and institutional barriers that prevented her from taking required courses. Rather than surrender, she petitioned the court for permission to attend an all-white school. Her courage opened doors, allowing her to become NASA's first Black female engineer and later an advocate for inclusion.

What Students Learn from the Women of Hidden Figures

Their collective journey teaches enduring lessons:

- Resilience thrives in excellence. Doing one's best can challenge unjust systems.
- Barriers do not define ability. Talent, determination, and preparation matter.
- Leadership includes lifting others. True resilience creates pathways, not walls.
- Advocacy is a form of courage. Speaking up changes systems.

Why This Story Matters for Today's Students

Student's today face obstacles that may feel invisible to others—bias, discouragement, self-doubt, or lack of opportunity. The women of Hidden Figures show that resilience is not always loud or confrontational. Sometimes it is steady, faithful, brilliant work done with dignity and perseverance.

Their legacy reminds us of a powerful truth: when resilience is combined with courage, knowledge, and unity, it has the power not only to change individual lives, but to alter the course of history.

The Liz Murray Story

Some stories remind us that resilience isn't born in comfort, but in the determination to rise when life feels impossible. The story of Liz Murray, often known as "Homeless to Harvard," stands as a powerful reminder that even in the most destabilizing circumstances, hope can take root, vision can grow, and a future can still be rewritten.

Liz grew up in New York City in a home marked by addiction, instability, and emotional pain. Both of her parents struggled with substance abuse. While other children returned to homes filled with routine, guidance, and structure, Liz returned to one marked by uncertainty, hunger, and chaos. Her childhood was not defined by opportunities but by survival.

School quickly faded from priority as life at home unraveled. By her early teens, Liz found herself without a stable place to live. After her mother died from complications related to AIDS and her father became unable to care for her, Liz became homeless. She slept in stairwells, on friends' couches, and on subway trains. She had every reason to give up. Many people in similar circumstances disappear into statistics.

FACING AND OVERCOMING ADVERSITY

Liz refused to let her life end in hopelessness. Standing on the edge of her circumstances, she made a decision that would change everything: she returned to high school—while homeless. Carrying her belongings in a bag, often exhausted and unsure where she would sleep at night, Liz chose education as an anchor. She completed four years of high school in just two years, earning top grades while navigating the daily trauma of homelessness.

Her resilience drew the attention of educators who believed in her potential. With the help of mentors and scholarship opportunities, Liz applied to Harvard University—and she was accepted. It wasn't a fairy-tale ending, but it was a powerful turning point. Liz didn't simply escape her past; she transformed it into purpose. She went on to share her journey globally, inspiring countless students, families, and educators with a message grounded in courage, dignity, and determination.

What Students Learn from Liz Murray

Liz's journey offers profound lessons for students and educators alike:

- Resilience is a daily decision. It is choosing hope again and again, even when circumstances say otherwise.

- Education can be a lifeline. School became stability, belonging, and possibility when life offered none.

- Support systems matter. Teachers, mentors, and compassionate adults help hold students when life is too heavy to hold alone.

- Your story does not define your future. Background does not equal destiny.

Why Her Story Matters for Today's Students

Many students silently carry trauma, instability, grief, and fear into classrooms every day. Liz Murray's story shows them that struggle does not disqualify them from greatness. It reminds educators that behind every disengaged face may be a story of survival—not laziness. Most importantly, it affirms that resilience is not perfection; it is persistence fueled by hope.

Liz Murray's life embodies a powerful truth: adversity may shape our beginnings, but resilience empowers us to rewrite the ending. Her journey reminds us that potential can survive hardship, purpose can rise from pain, and when compassion meets determination, extraordinary transformation is possible.

The Nelson Mandela Story

There are some lives that remind us that resilience is not only about enduring hardship—it is about transforming suffering into strength, anger into purpose, and injustice into a call to create a better world. Few leaders in history embody this kind of resilience more powerfully than Nelson Mandela.

Mandela was born in South Africa during a time when the system of apartheid stripped Black citizens of dignity, rights, and freedom. From a young age, he witnessed inequality not as something distant or theoretical, but as a daily reality shaping every aspect of life. Instead of accepting the world as it was, Mandela chose to become a voice for justice, equality, and human dignity.

That choice came at a cost. Mandela was arrested, separated from his family, labeled a threat, and eventually sentenced to life in prison. He spent 27 years behind bars, much of it in harsh conditions—breaking rocks, sleeping on a thin mat, and being allowed only limited visits and letters from loved ones. Prison could have broken his spirit, fueled bitterness, or silenced his hope.

Mandela made a different choice. Inside prison, he disciplined his mind and guarded his heart. He committed himself not to hatred, but to purpose. He studied, reflected, and strengthened his leadership. Rather than allowing prison to make him smaller, he allowed it to deepen his wisdom, strengthen his compassion, and sharpen his resolve. He once wrote that while jail could restrain his body, it could not restrain his belief in justice.

When Mandela was finally released after nearly three decades, the world expected revenge. Instead, Mandela chose reconciliation. He helped guide South Africa toward democracy, unity, and healing, becoming the nation's first Black president. He did not erase the truth of injustice, but he refused to let bitterness dictate the future. His resilience was not only survival—it was moral courage.

What Students Learn from Nelson Mandela

Mandela's journey offers profound lessons about resilience for students and educators:

- True resilience is rooted in purpose. When you stand for something meaningful, you can endure great hardship.
- Adversity can shape character rather than destroy it. Struggle can strengthen clarity, courage, and integrity.
- Forgiveness is a powerful expression of resilience. It takes strength to move forward without allowing anger to own your future.
- Leadership and resilience go hand in hand. Standing firm in values, even when it is costly, transforms communities—not just individuals.

Why His Story Matters for Today's Students

Student's today encounter injustice, discouragement, conflict, and moments when life feels unfair or overwhelming. Mandela's life teaches them that resilience is not passive—it is active, principled, and hopeful. It reminds them that strong character, patience, and commitment can outlast even the harshest circumstances.

Nelson Mandela's legacy teaches a defining truth: resilience is not just the capacity to endure hardship—it is the courage to rise from it with dignity, compassion, and purpose. His story reminds us that while adversity may shape our journey, it does not have to define our spirit.

The Florence Chadwick Story

Resilience is not only about strength; it is about vision—the ability to keep going when what you're reaching for is not yet visible. Few stories illustrate this more powerfully than the journey of Florence Chadwick, one of the world's greatest long-distance swimmers, whose life teaches students that sometimes the greatest barrier isn't the storm around us, but the doubt within us.

Florence Chadwick was no stranger to challenge. From an early age, she trained not in calm swimming pools, but in open water—where waves crash unpredictably, waters turn icy, and conditions constantly change. She dreamed not merely of swimming for medals, but of pushing human limits.

In 1952, Florence set out to swim from Catalina Island to the coast of California—a 26-mile swim through frigid water, strong currents, and heavy fog. As she swam, the fog grew so dense she could not see the coastline ahead. For hours she battled exhaustion, numbness, and uncertainty, unsure how much farther she had left. Surrounded by fog, unable to see success, worn down by fatigue, Florence finally stopped. She was pulled from the water. Only then did she learn the truth that she was less than one mile from the shore.

Later, reflecting on the moment, Florence said, "I'm not excusing myself, but if I could have seen the land, I know I could have made it." The barrier wasn't her strength. It wasn't the cold. It wasn't the distance. It was the fog.

Two months later, Florence returned to the same waters. The same cold. The same currents. The same physical pain. Only this time, she carried something different: a mental picture of the shore. Even though the fog was just as thick and she still could not see land, she kept reminding herself that the coastline was there. This time, she finished the swim.

Florence didn't just complete the journey—she set a world record, proving that when vision is stronger than discouragement, resilience prevails.

What Students Learn from Florence Chadwick

Florence's story powerfully reminds students and educators:

- Resilience requires vision. When you can't see the finish line, belief must carry you.
- Failure does not define you; it prepares you. Florence didn't quit her dream—she returned stronger.
- Mental resilience is as important as physical strength.
- Hope is a skill. Sometimes progress doesn't feel visible, but it is still happening.

Why Her Story Matters for Today's Students

Student's face "fog" all the time—uncertainty about academics, emotions, family challenges, grief, identity, and the future. They often grow discouraged not because they lack ability, but because they cannot "see" results yet. Florence Chadwick's story teaches them that resilience means believing in what you cannot yet see, trusting the process, and refusing to quit when life gets cloudy.

Her journey reminds us of a powerful truth: resilience is not just enduring the storm; it is holding onto the vision beyond it. When determination and hope stand stronger than doubt, ordinary people accomplish extraordinary things.

The Chaz Freeman Story

Yes, this is the story of my son. The son of Martin and Marshell Freeman.

Resilience is not only found in history books, heroic legends, or famous figures. Sometimes resilience lives closest to our hearts—in the quiet strength of those we love. The story of Chaz Freeman is one such powerful testimony. His life reminds us that resilience is not the absence of hardship, but the determination to keep living with purpose, joy, and faith when life changes without permission.

At age 35, when many people are settling into the familiar rhythms of adulthood, building careers, raising families, and planning futures, Chaz received a life-altering diagnosis: Multiple Sclerosis (MS). MS is not a short-term challenge. It is a lifelong condition that brings uncertainty, physical challenges, emotional weight, and moments of fear that cannot always be seen by others.

For many, a diagnosis like this can feel like the closing of doors—dreams paused, strength questioned, identity shaken. But Chaz chose a different response. Rather than allowing MS to define the boundaries of his life, he continued to define his life by passion, calling, and love. Today, Chaz is a professor of Writing at Rutgers University, shaping minds, guiding students, and continuing to do what he loves—teaching, thinking deeply, lifting others, and contributing meaningfully to the world of education. His diagnosis did not silence his voice. It did not steal his brilliance. It did not stop his purpose.

Even more beautifully, Chaz is not only a scholar and educator—he is a husband and father of three boys (Cristian, Cross, Cebastien). His wife Christa (also a special education teacher), has been his constant – his encourager, his anchor, and a steady presence reminding him he is never fighting alone.

His life is not defined by limitation, but by love, laughter, purpose, and presence. His resilience is not loud or theatrical. It shows up in everyday courage—showing up for his family, showing up for his students, showing up for himself.

Chaz's story reminds us that resilience is deeply human. It is waking up on days when the body feels heavy and choosing gratitude anyway. It is having every reason to retreat, yet continuing to participate fully in life. It is living with faith, hope, intelligence, humor, and dignity, even when the road is steep.

What Students Learn from the Story of Chaz Freeman

Chaz's journey speaks powerfully to students and educators:

- Resilience is not "getting over" something, but living well in the midst of it.
- Purpose gives strength. When you know why you live, you find the courage to continue.
- Family, community, and love matter. Support strengthens resilience.

- Adversity does not erase identity. You are still gifted. Still capable. Still called.

Why His Story Matters

For students who face health challenges, chronic conditions, invisible struggles, or unexpected life changes, Chaz's life testifies that their story is not over. Life may bend, but it does not have to break. Dreams may be challenged, but they do not have to disappear.

The story of Chaz Freeman teaches a profound truth: resilience is not just about surviving—it is about continuing to live with meaning, purpose, and heart. His life stands as a reminder that even when adversity walks beside us, hope, strength, and love can still lead the way.

Allow me to conclude with a spiritually rooted message of resilience. In seasons of strength and seasons of struggle, keeping God first anchors the heart in something greater than circumstances. When life feels uncertain, God provides stability. When challenges feel overwhelming, He offers peace that human strength cannot supply. Placing God first does not mean life becomes easy; it means we never face life alone. It shifts our perspective from fear to faith, from control to trust, from self-reliance to divine guidance.

Keeping God first reminds us that purpose does not end when adversity appears. It ground's identity not in what happens to us, but in who God says we are—loved, valued, capable, and never forgotten. It shapes decisions, strengthens character, deepens resilience, and fuels hope when emotions run empty. In every victory and every valley, prioritizing God keeps the soul centered, the mind steady, and the heart courageous.

To keep God first is not merely a spiritual discipline; it is a lifeline. It is choosing to trust His plan, lean on His grace, and believe that even in difficulty, He is working, sustaining, and building in each of us resilience.

Acknowledgements

I am deeply grateful to Superintendent Jeremy Batchelor for his valuable input and encouragement, the educators, leaders, parents, and students who inspired the vision behind this work. Special thanks to the district Scholar Advocates and Social Workers for their insight and partnership throughout this journey. At every staff meeting, I would hear the need as to why I should write this book. Heartfelt appreciation for my colleague and Pastor Garrick Matlock who heard my passion, and saw my tears writing this book. Thank you, Shaunda Yancey who reviewed my drafts for this manuscript. Finally, I thank my family for their patience, love, and unwavering belief in me.

About the Author

Martin Freeman (B.A., MABTS, Th.D., LSW) has served in Social Work, Education, and ministry for over 30 years.

Martin is currently employed with Youngstown City Schools where he serves as District Ombudsman. He has received the District Administrator or the Year Award in 2023, and the Anthony DeNiro Distinguished Service Award in 2024. Martin is a National Conference and motivational speaker.

Martin loves education, ministry, enjoys teaching, family, children, and is an avid golfer. Martin is the Author of his first published book "The Quest for Contentment," and his second book titled, "Incites to Excite: Inspiration for Everyday Living."

REFERENCES

Alvord, M. K., & Grados, J. J. (2005).Benzies & Mychasiuk, 2009; Fergus & Zimmerman, 2005; Martinez-Torteya, Bogat, von Eye, & Levendosky, 2009; Masten et al., 1991; Rak & Patterson, 1996; Walsh, 2003).Enhancing resilience in children: A proactive approach. Professional Psychology: Research and Practice, 36(3), 238–245, http://dx.doi.org/10. 1037/0735-7028.36.3.238.

Bandura, A. (1997). Self-efficacy: The exercise of control. New York, NY: W.H. Freeman.

Bath, H. (2008). The three pillars of trauma-informed care. Reclaiming Children and Youth, 17(3), 17–21.

Bath, H. (2008). Brunzell, T., Stokes, H., & Waters, L. (2016). Trauma-informed positive education: Using positive psychology to strengthen vulnerable students. Contemporary School Psychology, 20(1), 63–83.

Bethel CD, Newacheck P, Hawes E, Halton N. Adverse childhood experiences: assessing the impact on health and school engagement and the mitigating role of resilience. Health: Aff. 2014; 33 (12): 2106-2115. doi: 10.1377/dhlthaff.2014.091

Block, A. (2021). 5 Factors That Promote Resilience. Anti-Poverty Service-Learning Resources, University of Nebraska Omaha. https://digitalcommons.unomaha.edu/antipoverty/15.

Bhatnager, S. (2021). Rethinking stress resilience. *Trends in Neuroscience*, 44 (12), 936-945. https://doi.org/10.1016/j.tins.2021.09.005

National Scientific Council on the Developing Child. (2015). *Supportive relationships and active skill-building strengthen the foundations of resilience.* (Working Paper No. 13). Center on the Developing Child, Harvard University.

Compas, B., Jaser, S., Bettis, A., Watson, K., Gruhn, M., Dunbar, J., et al. (2017). Coping, emotion regulation, and psychopathology in childhood and adolescence. Journal of Child Psychology and Psychiatry, 58(4), 321–349.

Durlak, J., Weissberg, R., Dymnicki, A., Taylor, R., & Schellinger, K. (2011). The impact of enhancing students' social and emotional learning. Child Development, 82(1), 405–432.

Dweck, C. S., (2006). Mindset. The New Psychology of Success. New York, NY: Random House.

Esch, P., Bocquet, V., Pull, C., et al. (2014). The downward spiral of mental disorders and educational attainment. Social Psychiatry and Psychiatric Epidemiology, 49, 129-139.

Fergus, S., & Zimmerman, M. A. (2005). Adolescent resilience: A framework for understanding healthy development in the face of risk. Annual Review of Public Health, 26, 399–419, http://dx.doi.org/10.1146/annurev.publichealth.26.021304.144357

Furlong, M., O'Brennan, L., & You, S. (2011). Psychometric properties of the California school climate survey. Journal of Psychoeducational Assessment, 29(4), 273–287.

Garmezy, N. (1991) a. Resilience in children's adaptation to negative life events and stressed environments. Pediatric Annals, 20, 459-460, 463-466.4.

Goleman, D., (1995). Emotional Intelligence: Why it can matter more than IQ. New York, NY: Bantam Books.

Gwinn, C., & Hellman, C. (2018). Hope Rising: How the Science of Hope Can Change Your Life. Morgan James Publishing.

Hattie, J., & Timperley, H. (2007). The power of feedback. Review of Educational Research, 77(1), 81–112.

Jennings, P. & Greenberg, M. (2009). The prosocial classroom. Review of Educational Research, 79(1), 491–525.

Lopez, S. J., (2013). Making Hope Happen: Create the future you want for yourself and others. New York. Free Press.

Luthar, S. S., & Cicchetti, D. (2000). The construct of resilience: Implications for interventions and social policies. Development and Psychopathology, 12, 857–885.

Masten, A. S. (2001) Ordinary magic: Resilience processes in development. American Psychologist. 56, 227-238

Masten, A. S. (2014). Global perspectives on resilience in children and youth. Child Development, 85 (1), 6-20.

National scientific council on the developing child. (2015).

Noam, G. G., & Hermann, C. A. (2002). Where education and mental health meet: Developmental prevention and early intervention in schools. Development and Psychopathology, 14, 861–875

Perry, B. (2006). Applying principles of neurodevelopment to clinical work with maltreated children. In N. Boyd Webb (Ed.), Working with traumatized youth in child welfare.

Perry, B., & Szalavitz, M. (2006). The boy who was raised as a dog: And other stories from a child psychiatrist's notebook. New York, NY: Basic Books.

Rutter, M. 2006. Implications of resilience concepts for scientific understanding. Annals of the New York Academy of Sciences, 1094, 1-12.

Shonkoff, J. P., et al. (2012). The lifelong effects of early childhood adversity and toxic stress. Pediatrics, 129(1), e232-e246. https://doi.org/10.1542/peds.2011-2663

Skiba, R., Arrendondo, M., & Williams, N. (2014). Organizing for change in school discipline. Review of Research in Education, 38(1), 245-27

Snyder, C. R. (1994). The psychology of hope: You can get there from here. New York: Free Press.

Snyder, C. R. (2002). Hope theory: Rainbows in the mind. Psychological Inquiry, 13(4), 249–275. https//doi.org/10.1207/S15327965PLI1304-01

Sammons, P., Day, C., Kington, A., Gu, Q., Stobart, G., & Smees, R. (2007). Exploring variations in teachers' work, lives and their effects on pupils: Key findings and implications from a longitudinal study. British Educational Research Journal, 33(5), 681-701. https://doi.org/10.1080/01411920701582264

Southwick, S. M., Charney, D. S., Depierro, J. M., (2023). Resilience. The Science of Mastering Life's Greatest Challenges (p. 3)

Walsh, F. (2003). Family resilience: A framework for clinical practice. Family Process, 42(1), 1–18.

Weir, K. (2017, September, 1st). Maximizing Children's Resilience. Monitor on Psychology, Vol. 48. No 8. P. 40).

Werner, E. E. 1982. Vulnerable, but invincible: A longitudinal study of resilient children and youth. American Journal of Orthopsychiatric Association, 59.

Werner, E., & Smith, R. (2001). Journeys from childhood to midlife. Cornell University Press.

Yeager, D., & Dweck, C. (2012). Mindsets that promote resilience. Educational Psychologist, 47(4), 302–314.

Zimmerman, B. (2002). Ungar, M., (2015). Becoming a self-regulated learner. Theory Into Practice, 41(2), 64–70.*

www.ingramcontent.com/pod-product-compliance
Lightning Source LLC
LaVergne TN
LVHW012109070526
838202LV00056B/5677